Advanced Introduction to Corporate Venturing

Elgar Advanced Introductions are stimulating and thoughtful introductions to major fields in the social sciences and law, expertly written by the world's leading scholars. Designed to be accessible yet rigorous, they offer concise and lucid surveys of the substantive and policy issues associated with discrete subject areas.

The aims of the series are two-fold: to pinpoint essential principles of a particular field, and to offer insights that stimulate critical thinking. By distilling the vast and often technical corpus of information on the subject into a concise and meaningful form, the books serve as accessible introductions for undergraduate and graduate students coming to the subject for the first time. Importantly, they also develop well-informed, nuanced critiques of the field that will challenge and extend the understanding of advanced students, scholars and policy-makers.

For a full list of titles in the series please see the back of the book. Recent titles in the series include:

Post Keynesian Economics
J.E. King

International Intellectual Property
Susy Frankel and Daniel J. Gervais

Public Management and
Administration
Christopher Pollitt

Organised Crime
Leslie Holmes

The Law of International
Organizations
Jan Klabbers

International Environmental Law
Ellen Hey

International Sales Law
Clayton P. Gillette

Corporate Venturing
Robert D. Hisrich

Advanced Introduction to

Corporate Venturing

ROBERT D. HISRICH

Associate Dean of Graduate and International Programs, Bridgestone Chair of International Marketing, Kent State University, USA

with

DAVID W. KRALIK

Business Formation Advisor and Strategist, USA

Elgar Advanced Introductions

Edward Elgar
PUBLISHING
Cheltenham, UK • Northampton, MA, USA

Published by
Edward Elgar Publishing Limited
The Lypiatts
15 Lansdown Road
Cheltenham
Glos GL50 2JA
UK

Edward Elgar Publishing, Inc.
William Pratt House
9 Dewey Court
Northampton
Massachusetts 01060
USA

A catalogue record for this book
is available from the British Library

Library of Congress Control Number: 2016932477

ISBN 978 1 78254 648 1 (cased)
ISBN 978 1 78254 650 4 (paperback)
ISBN 978 1 78254 649 8 (eBook)

Typeset by Servis Filmsetting Ltd, Stockport, Cheshire
Printed and bound in Great Britain by TJ International Ltd, Padstow, Cornwall

To my spouse, Tina, children, Kary, Katy and Kelly, sons-in-law, Rich and Kevin, grandchildren, Andrew, Rachel and Sarah, and to David Kralik's best friend, Billy, a source of constant inspiration.

Contents

Preface   x
About the authors   xii

1 Corporate venturing: similarities and differences   1
   Scenario: Loctite Corporation   1
   An overview of entrepreneurship   3
   The entrepreneurial process   10
   The entrepreneurial process for each context   13
   A framework for corporate entrepreneurship   13
   Summary   15

2 Understanding corporate venturing and creative problem
   solving   17
   Scenario: Ericsson   17
   Aspects of corporate entrepreneurship   18
   Innovation   19
   Ownership   19
   Creativity and creative problem solving   20
   Change   24
   Summary   25

3 Innovation and identifying and evaluating the
   opportunities   27
   Scenario: Virgin Atlantic Airlines   27
   Creativity   29
   Innovation   31
   Design thinking   35
   Opportunity analysis plan   37
   Radical innovation   39
   Stage gate process   39
   Summary   40

4   Recognizing the opportunity for market disruption   42
    David W. Kralik
    Scenario: American Express   42
    Overview of market disruption   44
    Societal/macroeconomic indicators   46
    Trends brought about by changes in public policy   50
    Market share ownership indicators   55
    Summary   61

5   Developing the corporate business plan   66
    Scenario: Apple Inc.   66
    Introduction   69
    Importance of a business plan   69
    Scope and value of the business plan   70
    The corporate business plan   71
    Summary   86

6   Organizing corporate venturing   87
    Scenario: Textron Ltd   87
    Introduction   91
    Selecting a corporate entrepreneur and a team   91
    Corporate entrepreneurial team roles   99
    Key characteristics of the corporate entrepreneurial
        leader   99
    Survival guidelines for corporate entrepreneurs   100
    Venture life cycle and selection of the corporate
        entrepreneurial team   101
    Internal politics   102
    Overcoming the obstacles   104
    Political strategy   107
    Politics   108
    Political tactics for corporate entrepreneurs to increase
        their influence   109
    Political tactics for corporate entrepreneurs to exercise
        influence   110
    Summary   111

7   Controlling and compensating corporate venturing   113
    Scenario: Trojan Technologies   113
    Evaluating the corporate entrepreneurial team's
        performance   116
    Evaluation criteria for the corporate entrepreneurial team 116

Compensating corporate entrepreneurs   117
Components of a compensation and incentive system   119
Compensation and incentive components for new success   120
Summary   123

8 Implementing corporate venturing   **124**
Scenario: Tesla Motors   124
Models of corporate venturing   126
Specific examples of corporate venturing   129
Implementing and evaluating a corporate venturing
    program   136
Implementing   136
Benefits of a corporate entrepreneurship program   140
Evaluating the results   142
Summary   144

Index   145

Preface

Starting and operating a new business even under a corporate umbrella includes considerable risks and effort to overcome the inertia of creating something new of value both to the organization as well as the market and the individuals. In creating and growing a new corporate venture the corporate entrepreneur assumes the responsibility and risks for its development and survival.

To provide an understanding of this corporate venturing process this book is divided into eight chapters.

Chapter 1 (Corporate venturing: similarities and differences) provides an understanding of the similarities and differences between corporate entrepreneurship, entrepreneurship and social entrepreneurship. The nature of the entrepreneurial process is explained as well as its application in an organizational structure. The chapter concludes by introducing an overall framework for the book.

Chapter 2 (Understanding corporate venturing and creative problem solving) discusses the basic aspects of corporate venturing – innovation, ownership, creativity and change. Several methods useful for creative problem solving are discussed, as well as the attributes of an individual who is open minded and willing to change.

Chapter 3 (Innovation and identifying and evaluating the opportunities) discusses creativity, innovation and design thinking. The chapter concludes with a method for evaluating different opportunities – the opportunity analysis plan.

Chapter 4 (Recognizing the opportunity for market disruption) presents an overview of market disruption and its various aspects. Specific attention is given to markets that grow too fast or too slow as well as trends.

Chapter 5 (Developing the corporate business plan) presents an overview of the importance of a business plan as well as its scope and value. Following the discussion of the information needs for developing a good plan is a presentation of each of its aspects. The chapter concludes by presenting the use and implementation of the business plan and the reasons for failure.

Chapter 6 (Organizing corporate venturing) discusses the best ways to organize successful corporate venturing by first presenting a checklist for evaluating the potential of the idea in the organization. This is followed by a discussion of selecting a corporate entrepreneur and team, the roles of the team members, the impact of the venture life cycle, internal politics, and overcoming the obstacles they present, and political strategy and tactics.

Chapter 7 (Controlling and compensating corporate venturing) starts by presenting appropriate evaluation criteria for the corporate entrepreneurship team and project. Then the important issue of compensating the corporate entrepreneur is discussed along with the compensation and incentive components that motivates success.

Chapter 8 (Implementing corporate venturing), the final chapter, looks at the different models of corporate entrepreneurship. This is followed by presenting some specifics of the process. The chapter concludes with some ways to benchmark and evaluate the results.

Many people – business executives, corporate entrepreneurs, entrepreneurs, professors and students – have made many helpful suggestions that have made this book possible. Special thanks to David Kralik for authoring Chapter 4 and to Laxman Panthi for providing research material, editorial assistance and the final preparation of this manuscript. I am deeply indebted to my spouse Tina, children Kary, Katy and Kelly, sons-in law Rich and Kevin, grandchildren Andrew, Rachel and Sarah and Kaiya for providing the time and patience that went into the preparation of this book. May you always beg forgiveness than ask for permission.

Robert D. Hisrich

About the authors

Robert D. Hisrich is the Bridgestone Chair of International Marketing and Associate Dean of Graduate and International Programs at the College of Business Administration at Kent State University. He holds a BA from DePauw University and an MBA and a doctorate from the University of Cincinnati.

Professor Hisrich's research pursuits are focused on entrepreneurship and venture creation: entrepreneurial ethics; corporate entrepreneurship; women and minority entrepreneurs; venture financing; and global venture creation. He teaches courses and seminars in these areas, as well as in marketing management and product planning and development. His interest in global management and entrepreneurship resulted in two Fulbright Fellowships in Budapest, Hungary, honorary degrees from Chuvash State University (Russia) and the University of Miskolc (Hungary), and serving as visiting faculty member in universities in Austria, Australia, Ireland and Slovenia. Professor Hisrich serves on the editorial boards of several prominent journals in entrepreneurial scholarship, he is on several boards of directors and author or co-author of over 300 research articles appearing in journals such as the *Journal of Marketing, Journal of Marketing Research, Journal of Business Venturing, Journal of Developmental Entrepreneurship* and *Entrepreneurship Theory and Practice.* Professor Hisrich has authored or co-authored 40 books or their editions, including *Marketing: A Practical Management Approach* (1989), *How to Fix and Prevent the 13 Biggest Problems that Derail Business* (2004), *International Entrepreneurship: Starting, Developing and Managing a Global Venture* (3rd edition, 2015), *Technology Entrepreneurship: Value Creation, Protection, and Capture* (2nd edition, 2015) and *Entrepreneurship* (10th edition, 2016).

David W. Kralik is a Business Formation Advisor and Strategist with a global mindset. Using the lean startup methodology, he has advised dozens of award-winning companies. Prior to earning his MBA from the Thunderbird School of Global Management, he held various positions in politics, including Head of Strategy for former Speaker Newton 'Newt' Gingrich. His work has been profiled in the *Washington Post* and *Investor's Business Daily*. His work has also transcended pop culture, having been featured in a song by a platinum-award-winning musician, on an episode of *The Simpsons* and in *Playboy* magazine. In his spare time, he plays the saxophone and enjoys global travel, having travelled to all seven continents.

1 Corporate venturing: similarities and differences

While entrepreneurship has been discussed and researched for quite some time, other forms of entrepreneurship have had a more recent emergence. Governpreneurship, social entrepreneurship, technology entrepreneurship and corporate entrepreneurship, also labeled corporate venturing or intrapreneurship, is the focus of this book. This chapter introduces corporate venturing and its similarities and differences with the other types of entrepreneurship.

Scenario: Loctite Corporation

Loctite Corporation, the manufacturer of Super Glue, sells over 1,000 variations of high-technology sealants and coatings; the company markets its products to industrial and consumer markets in over 80 countries. While primarily Loctite's success stems from its consumer products, predominately Super Glue, the company derives the majority of its sales from industrial products used in diverse industrial applications, ranging from electronics to cosmetics.

Loctite Corporation (formally called American Sealants) was originally founded in 1953 by an American professor Vernon Krieble who developed anaerobic thread locking adhesives in his chemistry laboratory at Trinity College in Hartford, Connecticut. The products were patented as an entire system and aerobic sealants stored in Plax bottles was the pilot product. Retiring in 1955, Professor Krieble continued to develop the product and convinced a group of Trinity alumni to invest $100,000 to start production. In 1964, Loctite introduced 'Super Glue,' the first of many products, including silicones, acrylics and the development of new Loctite anaerobic. By 1965, Loctite sales had reached $2.8 million with a net income of $260,000.

In the mid 1970s, US automakers were producing smaller, lightweight vehicles, and Loctite's new product lines helped stop vibrations in their smaller, higher revving engines. Additional new products were developed in the early 1980s including a new generation micro anaerobic adhesive that did not activate until the parts were assembled. The most significant new product was Super Glue, developed by the company's labs in Ireland and Connecticut. Loctite also expanded its industrial product base through several key acquisitions including: (1) Permatex, an automotive line acquired in 1972, which had dressings that was a leader in the automotive repair market and (2) Woodhill Chemical Sales Company acquired in 1974, which had a line of adhesives for car and home repairs.

Loctite's Super Glue for wound closure dating back to 1970 was an excellent fast setting glue that bonded to skin and could be used as a wound closure glue to replace sutures in surgery. Since Loctite had no experience in medical products and no knowledge of this market, the product failed. In 1988, a professor from Leeds Bradford University doing research in adhesives in reconstruction surgery and wound healing developed with Loctite a 'Super Glue for Wound Closure' that could be sterilized. In 2002, the new product obtained (Food and Drug Administration [FDA]) approval.

The growth of various Loctite product lines as well as corporate acquisitions helped the company move into international markets. In many cases, companies were established separately by Loctite agents and eventually purchased by Loctite. In 1980, the company went public, merging with the International Sealants Corporation.

During the recession of the 1980s and 1990s, Loctite's sales were significantly impacted. Even though the consumer market of the company was strong, as most of Loctite's industrial sales were to overseas firms, the company became particularly vulnerable to fluctuations in the foreign currency rates. Even so, the company's ten-year annual earnings per share growth rate of 22.4 percent was the eighteenth highest among Fortune 500 companies.

In late 1996, the importance of adhesive and sealant activity in Europe took on greater significance. In 1997, Henkel KGaA, a German manufacturer of chemicals, detergents, industrial adhesives and cosmetics, acquired Loctite in a transaction valued at $1.2 billion. Combined with Henkel's adhesives, the Loctite acquisition made Henkel the largest adhesive company in the world.

An overview of entrepreneurship

The term 'entrepreneurship' means different things to different individuals. Several questions often asked are: Who is an entrepreneur? What is an entrepreneur? What is corporate entrepreneurship? What are corporate and social entrepreneurship? What is the entrepreneurial process? These frequently asked questions reflect the increased national and international interest in entrepreneurship by individuals, businesses, people, academics, students and government officials. The similarities and differences between three types of entrepreneurship – private, corporate and social – are indicated in Table 1.1.

Entrepreneurship definition

The development of the theory of entrepreneurship parallels to a large extent the development of the term itself. The word *entrepreneur* is French and literally translated means 'between-taker' or 'go-between.' An early example of this definition of an entrepreneur as a go-between is Marco Polo, who established trade routes to the Far East. In the Middle Ages, the term entrepreneur was used to describe both an actor and a person who managed large production projects. For example, a person in charge of such architectural works as castles, buildings or cathedrals was considered an entrepreneur. In these large production projects the individual did not take any risks, instead he managed the project using the resources provided by the government of the country.

In the seventeenth century, an entrepreneur was thought to be a person who entered into a contractual arrangement with the government to perform a service or supply products. For example, John Law, a Frenchman, was allowed to establish a royal bank. This monopoly on French trade led to Law's downfall when he attempted to push the company's stock price higher than the value of its assets leading to its collapse. Richard Cantillon, a noted economist and author in the 1700s, developed one of the early descriptions of an entrepreneur and is regarded by some as the founder of the term. He described the entrepreneur as a rational decision maker who assumed the risk and provided management for the firm. He viewed the entrepreneur as a risk taker.

In the eighteenth century, the entrepreneur was clearly distinguished from the capital provider. Eli Whitney and Thomas Edison developed

Table 1.1 Similarities and differences among private, corporate and social entrepreneurs and entrepreneurship

	Private entrepreneur/ entrepreneurship	Corporate entrepreneur/entrepreneurship	Social entrepreneur/entrepreneurship
Objectives	Requires freedom to discover and exploit profitable opportunities; independent and goal oriented; high need for achievement	Requires freedom and flexibility to pursue projects without being bogged down in bureaucracy; goal oriented; motivated but is influenced by corporate characteristics	Requires the freedom and resources to serve its constituencies; adds value to existing services; addresses social problems and enriches communities and societies; driven by desire for social justice
Opportunity	Pursues an opportunity regardless of the resources it controls; relatively unconstrained by situational forces	Pursues opportunities independent of the resources it currently controls; doing new things and departing from the customary to pursue opportunities	Shows a capacity to recognize and take advantage of opportunities to create social value by stimulating social change; develops a social value proposition to challenge equilibrium
Focus	Focuses strongly on the external environment; competitive environment and technological advancement; primary focus is on financial returns, profit maximization and independence	Focus on innovative activities and orientations such as development of new products, services, technologies, administrative techniques, strategies and competitive postures; primary focus is economic returns generated through innovation	Aims to create value for citizens by focusing on serving long-standing needs more effectively through innovation and creativity; aims to exploit social opportunities and enhance social returns, social wealth and social justice

Innovation	Creates value through innovation and seizing that opportunity without regard to either resources (human and capital); produces resources or endows existing resources with enhanced potential for creating wealth	A system that enables and encourages individuals to use creative processes that enable them to apply and invent technologies that can be planned, deliberate and purposeful in terms of the level of innovative activity desired; instigation of renewal and innovation within that organization	Creates practical, innovative and sustainable approaches to social problems for the benefit of society in general; mobilizes ideas and resources required for social transformation
Risk taking	Risk taking is a primary factor in the entrepreneurial character and function; assumes significant personal and financial risk but attempts to minimize it	Calculated risk taker; recognizes that risks are career related and absorbed by the organization as a whole	Recognises the social factor value creating opportunities and key decision-making characteristics of innovation, proactivity and risk taking; accepts an above average degree of risk
Character and skills	Self-confident; strong business knowledge; independent	Self-confident; strong self-belief that can manipulate the system; strong technical or product knowledge; good managerial skills	Self-confident; high tolerance for ambiguity; strong political skills

inventions during this time that were reactions to the needs of the changing world. While these inventors developed the new technologies, they were unable to finance their inventions by themselves. Whitney financed his cotton gin with expropriated British crown property. Edison raised capital from private sources to develop and experiment in the fields of electricity and chemistry. Both Edison and Whitney were capital users (entrepreneurs), not capital providers.

In the nineteenth and early twentieth centuries, entrepreneurs were frequently not distinguished from managers and were viewed mostly from an economic perspective. Some believed that the key factor in distinguishing a manager from an entrepreneur was the bearing of risk.[1] Andrew Carnegie is an example of this type of entrepreneur, as he did not invent anything, but rather adapted and developed new technology to create products of economic value in the steel industry.

In the middle of the twentieth century, the notion of an entrepreneur as an innovator was established in a more refined definition. The function of the entrepreneur was to: reform the pattern of production by exploiting an invention, develop a new technological method, open a new source of material supply or a new outlet for products, or organize a new industry.

The concept of innovation and newness became an integral part of entrepreneurship in the mid-twentieth century. Innovation, the act of introducing something new and relevant, is one of the most difficult tasks for the entrepreneur. It not only takes the ability to create and conceptualize, but also the ability to understand the environment. The newness can consist of anything from a new product or service, to a new distribution system, or a new method for developing a new organizational structure. Examples of these entrepreneurs include Edward Harriman, who reorganized the Ontario and Southern railroad through the North Pacific Trust and John Pierpont Morgan, who developed a large banking house for reorganizing and financing industries.

The term entrepreneurship has historically referred to the efforts of an individual taking on the odds to translate a vision into a successful business enterprise. While some definitions focus on the creation of new organizations, others focus on wealth creation and ownership, such as franchising, corporate entrepreneurship, management buyouts and business inheritance. Still other definitions focus on discovery and new opportunities.

The concept of an entrepreneur has been further refined from several different perspectives. From a personal perspective, the concept of entrepreneurship is viewed in terms of three behavioral attributes of an entrepreneur: (1) initiative taking; (2) organizing and reorganizing social and economic mechanisms to turn resources into value propositions and wealth; and (3) acceptance of the risk and possible failure.

From an economic perspective, an entrepreneur is one who combines resources, labor vision, materials and other assets to develop and create product or service value and/or introduce and implement change, innovation and a new order. From a psychological perspective, this person is typically driven by the need to attain something, to experiment, to accomplish or perhaps to escape authority. From a business perspective, an entrepreneur may appear as a threat, an aggressive competitor, an ally, a supplier, a customer or a creator of wealth.

Entrepreneurship is indeed a dynamic process of creating incremental wealth and stimulating the surrounding environment. The wealth is created by assuming the risks in terms of equity, time and career commitment to provide value in a product/service, which can have varying degrees of newness. Entrepreneurs of this century include Richard Branson, Michael Dell, Bill Gates, Steven Jobs and Anita Roddick.

While the perspectives have slightly different views for the entrepreneur, the descriptions also contain similar notions, such as newness, organizing, creating wealth and risk taking. These definitions are somewhat restrictive, since entrepreneurs are found in all professions – education, medicine, research, law, architecture, engineering, social work, distribution and government. To include all types of entrepreneurial behavior, there is a need for an all-inclusive definition as follows: 'Entrepreneurship is the process of creating something new with value by devoting the necessary time and effort assuming the accompanying financial, psychic, and social risks and uncertainties.'[2]

Corporate entrepreneurship

The challenge facing organizations today is recognizing the creativity and innovative capability of their internal members and allowing these individuals to have the ability to utilize their potential. Corporate entrepreneurship, sometimes referred to as intrapreneurship, or corporate venturing or organizational entrepreneurship, is the process by which individuals in organizations pursue opportunities independent of the resources they currently control; this usually involves doing new things and departing from the customary to pursue opportunities. The spirit of entrepreneurship within an existing organization results in the creation of a new organization, or in the development of innovation within that organization. Corporate entrepreneurship requires engendering entrepreneurial behaviors within an established organization. This enables individuals to use creative processes for applying and inventing technologies as well as new ways of doing things.

Corporate venturing involves extending the organization's competence and doing things through internally generated new resource combinations. Profit-making innovations can be fostered by encouraging employees to think like entrepreneurs and then giving them the freedom and flexibility to pursue projects without being inhibited by bureaucratic barriers. Companies such as IBM recognized the value of corporate venturing in increasing corporate growth. Hewlett-Packard (HP), 3M, Apple Inc. and Xerox have also experienced significant success in corporate venturing. Entrepreneurship can also be indirectly encouraged as in the case of Starlight Telecommunications, which was the successful result of lack of support by GTE making William O'Brien and Pete Nielson resign and start this new firm.

A broad definition of corporate entrepreneurship was proposed by Ginsberg and Guth who stressed that corporate entrepreneurship encompasses two major phenomena: new venture creation within existing organizations and the transformation of organizations through strategic renewal.[3] This renewal involves either formal or informal activities aimed at creating new businesses or processes in established companies at the corporate, division (business), functional or project level. The ultimate aim of the renewal is to improve the company's competitive position and financial performance. Renewal is achieved through the redefinition of an organization's mission by the creative redeployment of resources, leading to new combinations of products and technologies.

Social entrepreneurship

While the term entrepreneurship is mostly associated with for-profit activity, in the last 20 years the value creation aspect of entrepreneurship has been extended to non-profit social organizations. Social entrepreneurship has made significant contributions to communities and society by adopting business models to develop innovative and creative solutions for complex social issues. The increased interest in social entrepreneurship and impact of social entrepreneurship is evidenced by the *Fast Company Magazine*'s Social Capitalist Awards and the Skoll Foundations Award for Social Entrepreneurship.

One challenge is that the definition of social entrepreneurship has been developed in a number of different domains such as not-for-profits, for-profits, public sector organizations and a combination of the three. Social entrepreneurship can be broadly defined as any innovative activity with a social objective in the for-profit sector such as social commercial ventures, non-profit sector, public sector or even across sectors in terms of hybrid organizations, which often combine for-profit and non-profit approaches. While there are other definitions of social entrepreneurship, common across all definitions is that its core objective is to create social value, rather than personal and stakeholder wealth.

Even though the above definitions of private entrepreneurship, corporate entrepreneurship and social entrepreneurship have a slightly different perspective, they contain similar concepts involving creative activity in the discovery and exploitation of opportunities. No entrepreneurial event can occur without identifying and addressing an opportunity.

As previously indicated, Table 1.1 depicts a typology that identifies the similarities and differences between these three types of entrepreneurship and entrepreneurs are characterized as having a preference for creative activity with some degree of proactiveness and innovativeness. The core of entrepreneurship involves the discovery and exploitation of opportunities.

Entrepreneur versus manager

Sometimes there is confusion about the similarities and differences of an entrepreneur and a manager. Although the entrepreneur is different from the traditional manager, entrepreneurship represents a mode of management. Management is involved in achieving the objectives of an organization while reducing variability and increasing stable processes. It involves accomplishing work through people. To manage effectively means to forecast, plan, organize, coordinate, communicate, lead, facilitate, motivate and control. Managers need to be efficient (doing things right) and effective (doing the right things) in utilizing resources to achieve optimum results in line with organizational goals and objectives.

An entrepreneur is future oriented, seeking opportunities and identifying innovations to fill these opportunities. An entrepreneur prefers creative activity, manifested by some innovative combination of resources, for achieving financial, economic or social wealth. Entrepreneurs are creative in obtaining resources, overcoming obstacles and implementing ideas. While there is considerable overlap between managers and entrepreneurs, the concepts are not the same; entrepreneurs can be mangers and mangers entrepreneurs by consciously combining the various functions of the key roles at the appropriate times.

The entrepreneurial process

The entrepreneurial process involves more than just problem solving. A private entrepreneur/corporate entrepreneur/social entrepreneur must find, evaluate and develop an opportunity by overcoming all the forces that resist the creation of something new. Understanding how entrepreneurship works requires recognition of the process involved and how to effectively manage it. It is a process that can occur in different settings with changes reflecting the diversity that exists between private, corporate and social contexts.

The entrepreneurial process has four distinct phases: (1) identification and evaluation of the opportunity; (2) development of the business plan; (3) determination and evaluation of resource requirements; and (4) implementation and management of the resulting enterprise. Table 1.2 indicates the various steps in the entrepreneurial context. Although these phases precede progressively, no one stage occurs in isolation or is completely done before work begins on other phases. For example, to successfully identify and evaluate an opportunity (phase 1), an entrepreneur must already have in mind the type of desired business (phase 4).

Identification and evaluation of the opportunity

Opportunity identification and evaluation is a most difficult task. Entrepreneurship does not always begin with the creative concept for a new product, service or process. It often begins with the entrepreneur's alertness to an opportunity. Whether the opportunity is identified by

Table 1.2 The entrepreneurial process: entrepreneur context

Identify and evaluate the opportunity	Develop the business plan	Determine and evaluate resource requirements	Launch and manage the enterprise
Opportunity assessment	Title page	Determine needed resources	Develop management style
Creation and length of opportunity	Table of contents	Determine existing resources	Understand key variables for success
Real and perceived value of opportunity	Executive summary		
	Major sections:		
	1. Description of business	Identify resource gaps and available suppliers	Identify problems and potential problems
Risk and returns of opportunity	2. Description of industry		
	3. Technology plan		
	4. Marketing plan		
Opportunity versus personal skills and goals	5. Financial plan	Develop access to needed resources	Implement control systems
	6. Production plan		
	7. Organizational plan		Develop growth strategies
Competitive environment	8. Operational plan		

using input from consumers, business associates, channel members or technical experts, it needs to be carefully screened and evaluated. The evaluation of the opportunity is perhaps the most critical aspect of the entrepreneurial process as it assesses whether the specific product or service has the necessary returns compared to the required resources as well as other opportunities. Offering a better product, service or process at a lower price with higher quality, greater availability and better customer and after sales service means nothing if a large enough market does not exist.

The evaluation process involves looking at the length of the opportunity, its real and perceived value, its risks and returns, its fit with personal skills and goals of the entrepreneur (or the organization that the corporate entrepreneur or social entrepreneur is part of) and its uniqueness or different advantage in the environment. The entrepreneur, corporate entrepreneur or social entrepreneur must believe in the opportunity to such an extent that they will make the necessary sacrifices in order to overcome any potential personal or organizational obstacles to develop and manage the opportunity.

Key issues for the private entrepreneur, corporate entrepreneur or social entrepreneur include: a description of the product, service, process; an assessment of the opportunity in terms of source, size and sustainability; an assessment of the entrepreneur and the team; specifications of all the activities and resources needed to translate the opportunity into a viable business venture; and the source of capital to finance the initial venture as well as its growth.

Development of the business plan

Once the opportunity is identified and evaluated, the private entrepreneur/corporate entrepreneur/social entrepreneur needs to specify the business concept. The business concept for a new product, service or process specifies the innovative and creative approach for capitalizing on the opportunity. A good business plan needs to be developed to capture the defined opportunity. This is a time-consuming phase of the entrepreneurial process and varies according to the context. For example, the business plan for an entrepreneurial start-up is different from the corporate entrepreneur business plan, which is different from the social entrepreneur business plan (see Tables 1.1 and 1.2). A good business plan is needed for capturing the opportunity and determining the required resources, obtaining those resources and successfully starting and managing the resulting venture.

Determine and evaluate resource requirements

The private entrepreneur/corporate entrepreneur/social entrepreneur needs to determine the resources needed for addressing the opportunity. This process starts with the appraisal of the present financial and non-financial (for example, technical skills, team competencies, licenses, patents, customer contacts, location) resources. Care needs to be taken to avoid underestimating the amount of variety of resources needed. While for the corporate entrepreneur, sponsorship from a senior executive might be the most valuable resource, for the social entrepreneur government support might be a more significant resource. Some of the most critical entrepreneurial behaviors involve leveraging resources that allow concepts to move toward development without major financial commitments and providing greater flexibility to utilize resources only when needed.

Starting and managing the resulting enterprise

After resources are acquired, the private entrepreneur/corporate entrepreneur/social entrepreneur needs to implement the business plan and start operations of the venture. For the private entrepreneur, this involves implementing a management style and structure, whereas the corporate entrepreneur and social entrepreneur need to adapt and overcome restrictions or limitations. A control system needs to be implemented in order to quickly identify and resolve any problems occurring. Some private entrepreneurs thrive during the creation stage but have difficulty managing and growing the venture. In comparison, some corporate entrepreneurs/social entrepreneurs have difficulty managing their innovations because of organizational restrictions and limitations.

The private entrepreneur/corporate entrepreneur/social entrepreneur needs to be able to tolerate risk, uncertainty and ambiguity by adapting and adjusting accordingly. Ultimately, their mindset needs to rapidly sense, act and mobilize even under uncertain conditions. They need to be dynamic, flexible and engaged in the process of generating multiple decision frameworks to sense and react to any changes in the environment.

The entrepreneurial process for each context

While entrepreneurship is a universal concept, successfully applying the entrepreneurial process within private start-ups, established organizations or social enterprises requires appreciating the uniqueness of each one and adapting the process. The four stages of the entrepreneurial process apply within all contexts as the same stages occur for the corporate or social entrepreneur. In all instances, opportunities need to be identified and evaluated, innovative concepts need to be planned, resources need to be evaluated and ideas need to be managed and implemented within a specified timeframe.

A framework for corporate entrepreneurship

Like many entrepreneurs who find it difficult to manage and expand the venture created, many managers find it difficult to allow employees to innovate and engage in venturing activities. In order to develop and

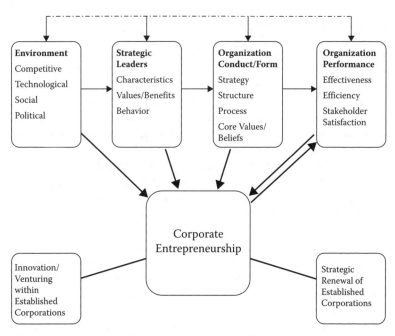

Figure 1.1   Framework of corporate entrepreneurship

grow the organization, managers need to be more entrepreneurial by building and developing an organization that encourages corporate entrepreneurial behavior and reward employees for taking creative risks.

Ginsberg and Guth have discussed a model to fit corporate entrepreneurship into strategic management (Figure 1.1). They present the various factors influencing corporate entrepreneurship and how the process of corporate entrepreneurship affects the performance of the firm.[4]

Never before has there been such a need for corporate entrepreneurship as organizations face increased, almost hyper, competition from globalization and rapid technology. Since customers have access to most product and service substitutes today, a firm's competition can be anywhere in the world. There is a pressing need for organizations to stay competitive by becoming more innovative and engaging in more corporate venturing activities. Leading international corporate entrepreneurship companies include 3M, Lucent Technologies, Nokia, Siemens, Nixdorf, DuPont and Apple Computers.

This book advances the concept of corporate venturing by discussing the aspects of corporate entrepreneurship and how to establish an entrepreneurial spirit in the organization. An integrative framework to advanced entrepreneurship has been developed.

The starting point is to develop an understanding of managing corporate entrepreneurship. Since entrepreneurship is a universal concept, there are certain commonalities regardless of the context; there are also fundamental differences when attempting to apply 'entrepreneurship' in a large corporation or social enterprise. An organizational environment needs to be created that encourages and motivates employees to identify and recognize opportunities and to behave more like entrepreneurs. Four key elements for managing corporate entrepreneurship and venturing include: understanding entrepreneurship and corporate entrepreneurship within different contexts; recognizing the behavioral aspects of corporate entrepreneurship; formatting and managing the venturing process with the structure in place; and effectively managing the opportunity identification, evaluation and selection process.

The ability to effectively manage the venture requires proper organization, which includes proper location of the venture, organization of resources and controlling and managing the internal politics. Finally, operationalizing corporate entrepreneurship requires a clear understanding and development of the business plan, selecting the right management, and compensating them for their efforts, ensuring adequate funding and instituting the concept of organizational structure.

The starting point for this book is to understand the aspects of corporate entrepreneurship. Then how to identify opportunities and develop a business plan are discussed. Following this is a discussion of the important areas of corporate entrepreneurship: selecting and compensating corporate entrepreneurs and financing the process and resulting venture. The book concludes with a chapter on implementing the corporate venturing process in light of the internal politics of the corporation.

Summary

The terms *entrepreneur* and *entrepreneurship* have various meanings to different people and can be viewed in different contexts such as private sector entrepreneurship, corporate entrepreneurship and venturing and social entrepreneurship. In spite of the differences, some similarities like risk taking, creativity, independence and reward are apparent.

The private entrepreneur/corporate entrepreneur/social entrepreneur proceeds through the entrepreneurial process by identifying, evaluating and developing opportunities for creating a venture. Each step is essential to eventual success. In established organizations, a corporate imperative is to achieve equilibrium between the role of management and the role of the entrepreneur, thus developing entrepreneurial managers.

The challenge for private entrepreneurs/corporate entrepreneurs/ social entrepreneurs is to build organizations for today's output and tomorrow's innovation. An organization needs to have sufficient internal diversity in strategies, structures, people and processes to facilitate different kinds of entrepreneurial behavior. Within existing corporate structures, the corporate entrepreneur needs to be creative, visionary and flexible and have the ability to work within the corporate structure. This type of corporate venturing will create long-term, sustained economic and social wealth and help ensure the future growth and development of the organization.

NOTES

1 John Stuart Mill, *Principles of Political Economy with Some of their Applications to Social Philosophy*, London: Longman, 1848, pp. 45–60.

2 Robert D. Hisrich, Michael P. Peters and Dean A. Shepard, *Entrepreneurship* (8th edn), Chicago: McGraw-Hill/Irwin, 2010, pp. 6–10.

3 Ari Ginsberg and William Guth, 'Guest Editors' Introduction,' *Corporate Entrepreneurship. Strategic Management Journal*, **11**, 1990, 5–15, specifically pp. 5–6.

4 Ibid., p. 7.

Online sources

http://www.loctite.com.

http://www.loctiteproducts.com.

http://www.fundinguniverse.com/company-histories/Loctite-Corpopration-Company-History.html.

2 Understanding corporate venturing and creative problem solving

A key aspect of successful corporate venturing is to instill a behavioral culture that supports creativity and innovation. It is important to understand both components of the creative process as well as some of the creative problem-solving techniques that can be used.

Scenario: Ericsson

Ericsson, a recognized leader in the telecommunications industry since 1876, is a worldwide provider of telecommunications equipment and related services to mobile and fixed network operators. Its founder, Lars Magnus Ericsson, decided to open a production facility in Russia in the early days of the company. Since technology and innovation are so important and a driver at the company, Ericsson uses a market-driven innovation strategy, focusing on making available technology, locally customized, adapted to meet local customer expectations.

In brief, in 1900, when Ericsson employed 1,000 people globally and produced 50,000 telephones, switches were put into service; in 1950, LM Ericsson telephone exchange (AXE) was installed; in 1991, AXE lines exceeded 105 million in 11 countries serving 34 million subscribers; in 2000, the company became the world's leading supplier of 3G mobile systems; in 2005, Ericsson won the biggest contract to date to manage Operator 3's networks in Italy and the United Kingdom; in 2008, a research center was established in Silicon Valley; and in 2009, Verizon and Ericsson collaborated to carry out the first call on a 4G network. Ericsson has a long history of innovation and pioneering the next generation technologies for more efficient and higher quality communications. In 1878, Ericsson introduced telephones with a simple trumpet; in 1968, the first digital telephone exchange (AXE) was installed; in 1981, the first mobile system, Nordic Mobile Telephone (NMT), was inaugurated in Saudi Arabia; in 1991, the first global system for mobile communication (GSM) phones was introduced; in 1999, Ericsson pushed for 3G and mobile internet; in 2003, high-speed broadband (wideband code division multiple access, WDCMA) rollout started globally; in 2007, full service broadband, with fixed and wireless coverage, was introduced; in 2008; Ericsson pushed for 4G (Long-term evolution, LTE), the standard the company help to form; in 2009, Ericsson won the IEC InfoVision Award for fiber and backhaul solutions. In 2011, Ericsson completed the acquisition of Telcordia. Recently, in 2013, Ericsson launched the Ericsson Radio Dot System that enables mobile operators to deliver consistently high-performance voice and data coverage and capacity in the broadest range of enterprise buildings and public venues.

The company continually innovated, being a market leader in such areas as providing the first 500 point-switches, the first international call, managing Operator 3's network in Italy, the first data call on a 4G network, the first digital telephone exchange (AXE) and a high-speed broadband and full service broadband with fixed and wireless network convergence. Since their award, Ericsson has networks in more than 200 countries, is a principal supplier of global networks and has strong research and development competencies with over 3,000 patents. The company has a strong market position and has become a unique player in the industry. This has been achieved through wireless, optical and wireline products. As a result of the combination of innovative ideas and network convergence technologies, LG-Ericsson provides the connectivity that eliminates barriers in the exchange of information, enabling customers to recognize user's potential.

Aspects of corporate entrepreneurship

While the specific aspects of corporate entrepreneurship vary from organization to organization, four common aspects are indicated in the formula below:

$$L = I + O + Cr + Ch$$

Where L = Level of entrepreneurship, I = Innovation, O = Ownership, Cr = Creativity and Ch = Change.

Each of these four aspects – innovation, ownership, creativity and change – are discussed in turn.

Innovation

While innovation is highly valued and a central aspect of most organizations, few organizations are satisfied with the return on their spending. According to a survey on corporate innovation by the Boston Consulting Group, which drew responses from about 3,000 global executives, innovation is at or near the top of the company's agenda with 43 percent of the respondents considering it one of their three most important strategic priorities and 23 percent considering it their top priority. In spite of its priority, satisfaction with the return on innovation spending continues to decrease.

Ownership

Ownership is also an important aspect of corporate entrepreneurship reflecting the overall organizational environment or culture. Ownership refers to owning and feeling responsible for one's job and having the desire to perform the job in the most efficient and effective manner possible; this is indicated in their love to go to work.

The overall characteristics of a good corporate entrepreneurial environment encourages ownership. First, since research and development is a key source for successful ideas, the firm needs to operate on the cutting edge of the industry's technology. New ideas need to be encouraged and supported, not always requiring these to have a rapid return on investment and a high sales volume.

Second, experimentation with trial and error needs to be encouraged. Successful new products/services rarely just appear fully developed; instead they evolve requiring time, effort, company support and money. It took time and some product failures before the first marketable computer appeared. A company wanting to establish a corporate entrepreneurial spirit has to establish an environment that allows mistakes and failures in developing new and innovative products/services. These failures need to be viewed as an indirect investment for creating the successful innovative products.

Third, the organization needs to make sure there is no initial opportunity parameters inhibiting creativity in the new product development process employed. Frequently in an organization some 'turfs' are protected, frustrating attempts by potential corporate entrepreneurs to establish new ventures. In one Fortune 500 company, an attempt to establish a corporate entrepreneurial environment eventually failed when the potential corporate entrepreneurs were informed that a proposed new product and venture was not possible because it was in the domain of another division.

Fourth, the resources of the firm need to be available and accessible, supporting the corporate entrepreneurship process. As one corporate entrepreneur stated, 'if my company really wants me to take the time, effort and career risks to establish a new venture, then it needs to put resources on the line.' Often, insufficient funds are allocated not in creating something new but in solving problems that have an immediate effect on the bottom line. Some companies – like Xerox, 3M, Apple and Intel – have recognized this problem and established separate venture capital areas for funding new internal as well as external ventures. Besides encouraging teamwork, a long time horizon for evaluating the success of the overall program as well as the success of each individual venture needs to be established. This patient attitude is similar to the investment–return expectation of venture capitalists and others when they invest in an entrepreneurial effort.

The fifth characteristic establishes a volunteer (not forced) process and an appropriate reward system. The corporate entrepreneur needs to be appropriately rewarded for all the energy, effort and risk taking expended in the creation of the new venture. Rewards should be based on the attainment of established goals and are discussed in Chapter 7.

Finally, and perhaps most importantly, the corporate entrepreneurial activity must be wholeheartedly supported and embraced by members of top management, by their physical presence and by their making sure that the personnel and financial resources are available. Sponsors and champions need to be throughout the organization. Without top management support, a successful environment cannot be created.

Creativity and creative problem solving

The third aspect of successful corporate entrepreneurship is creativity. While creativity and innovation are discussed in Chapter 3, some aspects, particularly creative problem-solving techniques, are presented in this chapter as this is the most important part of corporate entrepreneurship. Creativity – the ability to bring into being from one's imagination something unique and original – is very important and yet often lacking in many organizations.

Unfortunately, creativity tends to decline with age, education, lack of use and bureaucracy. Creativity generally declines in stages, beginning when a person starts school. It continues to deteriorate through the teens and continues to progressively decrease through ages 30, 40 and 50. Also, the latent creative potential of an employee can be stifled by perceptual, cultural, emotional and organizational factors. Creativity generally can be unlocked and creative ideas and innovations generated by using some creative problem-solving technique.

Brainstorming

The first technique, brainstorming, is probably the most well known and widely used for both creative problem solving and idea generation. In creative problem solving, brainstorming can generate ideas about a problem within a limited timeframe through spontaneous contributions of participants. A good brainstorming session starts with a problem statement that is neither too broad (which would diversify ideas too greatly so that nothing specific would emerge) nor too narrow (which would tend to confine responses). Once the problem statement is prepared, usually eight to 12 individuals are selected to participate. To avoid inhibiting responses, no group member should be a recognized expert in the field of the problem or product area as their presence would decrease participation. All ideas, no matter how illogical, need to be recorded, with participants prohibited from criticizing or evaluating during the brainstorming session.

Reverse brainstorming

Reverse brainstorming is similar to brainstorming except that criticism is allowed. In fact, the technique is based on finding fault by asking the question: 'In how many ways can this idea fail?' Since the main focus is based on the negative aspects of a product, a service or idea, care must be taken to maintain a group's morale. Reverse brainstorming can be effectively used better than other creative techniques to stimulate innovative thinking.[1] The process usually involves the identification of everything wrong with an idea, followed by a discussion of ways to overcome these problems. Reverse brainstorming almost always produces some worthwhile results as it is easier for an individual to be critical about an idea than to come up with a new idea.

Gordon method

The Gordon method, unlike other creative problem-solving techniques, begins with members not knowing the exact nature of the problem. This ensures that the solution is not closed to preconceived ideas and behavioral patterns.[2] The entrepreneur starts by mentioning a general concept associated with the problem. The group responds by expressing a number of ideas. Then a concept is developed, followed by related concepts, through guidance by the entrepreneur. The actual problem is then revealed, enabling the group to make suggestions for implementation or refinement of the final solution.

Checklist method

In the checklist method, a new idea is developed through a list of related issues and suggestions. The entrepreneur can use the list for questions or statements to guide the direction of developing entirely new ideas or concentrating on specific 'idea' areas. The checklist may take any form and be of any length. One general checklist is as follows:[3]

- Put to other uses? New ways to use as-is? Other uses if modified?
- Adapt? What else like this? What other ideas does this suggest? Does past offer parallel? What could I copy? Whom could I emulate?
- Modify? New twist? Change meaning, color, motion, odor, form, shape? Other changes?
- Magnify? What to add? More time? Greater frequency? Stronger? Larger? Thicker? Extra value? Plus ingredient? Duplicate? Multiply? Exaggerate?
- Minify? What substitute? Smaller? Condensed? Miniature? Lower? Shorter? Lighter? Omit? Streamline? Split up? Understand?
- Substitute? Who else instead? What else instead? Other ingredient? Other material? Other process? Other power? Other place? Other approach? Other tone of voice?
- Rearrange? Interchange components? Other pattern? Other layout? Other sequence? Transpose cause and effect? Change track? Change schedule?
- Reverse? Transpose negative and positive? How about opposites? Turn it backward? Turn it upside down? Reverse roles? Change shoes? Turn tables? Turn other check?
- Combine? How about a blend, an alloy, an assortment, an ensemble? Combine units? Combine purposes? Combine appeals? Combine ideas?

Forced relationships

Forced relationships force relationships among some product combinations. It is a technique that asks questions about objects or ideas in an effort to develop a new idea. The new combination and eventual concept is developed through a five-step process:

1. Isolate the elements of the problem.
2. Find the relationships between these elements.
3. Record the relationships in an orderly form.
4. Analyse the resulting relationships to find ideas or patterns.
5. Develop new ideas from these patterns.

Table 2.1 illustrates the use of this technique with paper and soap.

Collective notebook method

In the collective notebook method, a small notebook that easily fits in a pocket – containing a statement of the problem, blank pages and any pertinent background data – is distributed. Participants consider the problem and its possible solutions, recording ideas at least once, but preferably three times, a day. At the end of the week, a list of the best ideas is developed, along with any suggestions.[4] This technique can also be used with a group of individuals who record their ideas, giving their notebooks to a central coordinator who summarizes all the material and lists the ideas in order of frequency of mention. The summary becomes the topic of a final creative focus group discussion by the participants.

Table 2.1   Illustration of forced relationship technique

Elements: Paper and Soap

Forms	Relations/combination	Idea/pattern
Adjective	Papery Soap	Flakes
	Soapy Paper	Wash and dry travel aid
Noun	Paper soaps	Tough paper impregnated with soap and useable for washing surfaces
Verb	Soaped papers	Booklet of soap leaves
correlates	Soap 'wets' paper	In coating and impregnation process
	Soap 'cleans' paper	Suggests wallpaper cleaner

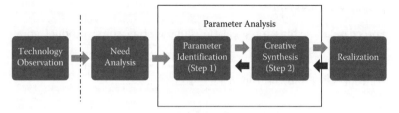

Figure 2.1   Illustration of parameter analysis

Attribute listing

Attribute listing is an idea-finding technique that requires the participants to list the attributes of an item or problem and then look at each from a variety of viewpoints. Through this process, originally unrelated objects can be brought together to form a new combination and possible new uses that better satisfy a need.

Parameter analysis

A final method for developing a new idea – parameter analysis – involves two aspects: parameter identification and creative synthesis. As indicated in Figure 2.1, step one (parameter identification) involves analyzing variables in the situation to determine their relative importance. These variables become the focus of the investigation, with other variables being set aside. After the primary issues have been identified, the relationships between parameters that describe the underlying issues are examined. Through an evaluation of the parameters and relationships, one or more solutions are developed; this solution development is called creative synthesis.

Change

In order for corporate entrepreneurship to thrive in an organization, the final 'C' of the formula – change – needs to be continuously allowed and encouraged. Organizational change should ideally be allowed and encouraged. Organizational change is often the result of an accumulation of smaller steps (changes) taken over time. Adam Smith in his *Theory of Moral Sentiments* referred to this as 'gradual greatness.' People tend to be more accepting of change if they can see and experience the steps slowly. New technologies, strategies, structures and/or rapid business expansion originate from smaller experimental steps and reflect the transference of knowledge and continual practice in the organization.

The idea that change in an organization should occur incrementally and collectively rather than suddenly suggests that an entrepreneurial organization should be continually experimenting and modifying around the edges of its core business. Change, discovery and renewal are fundamental aspects of this type of organization. As this becomes more apparent, managers are encouraged to develop creative, individualistic approaches and unexpected solutions to problems. This leads to charismatic individual leadership and inventive, creative decision making. It might be necessary, in order to start this process, to let go some of the existing managers who neither possess the skills nor desire to develop them.

It is important for changes to occur and be implemented to first establish a sense of urgency and form a strong guiding coalition. Since an organization is focused on short-term results without establishing the need for change due to the external environment and competitive landscape, the appropriate timeframe will not be established. And if a group is not established that has enough power and credibility, nothing will be implemented.

The group needs to establish a vision and strategic plan and communicate this throughout the organization by every means possible. Following the identification and selection of a champion, limit the obstacles, establish the appropriate new system and reward all creative thinking. The next step is to ensure to the extent possible that the first initiatives are successful with visible performance improvements. This will make failures easier to handle when they occur, which they will. It is easier to be successful at smaller changes than larger ones. Eventually, the new changes need to be consolidated; producing still more changes and allowing the change approach and change attitude to be institutionalized in the organization.

Summary

This chapter has focused on understanding and managing the corporate venturing process. Attention is paid to the four aspects of the corporate entrepreneurial process – identifying and evaluating the opportunity, developing a business plan, determining the resources required and starting and managing the venture. This corporate entrepreneurial process needs to be modified for specific corporate cultures in order to facilitate corporate entrepreneurship. The differences between managerial and corporate entrepreneurial decision making are discussed in terms of five business decisions – strategic orientation, commitment to opportunity, commitment to resources, control of resources and management structure. Following a discussion about the reasons for the increasing interest in corporate venturing, the differences between a corporate and a corporate entrepreneurial culture are presented.

The four major aspects of corporate entrepreneurship in an organization are then articulated – innovation, ownership, creativity and change and include a discussion of some of the most frequently used methods in a company to generate creativity – brainstorming, reverse brainstorming, Gordon method, checklist method, collective notebook method, forced relationships and parameter analysis.

NOTES

1 For a discussion technique, see J. Geoffrey Rawlinson, *Creative Thinking and Brainstorming*, New York: John Wiley & Sons, 1981, pp. 124, 126; and W.E. Souder and R.W. Ziegler, 'A review of creativity and problem-solving techniques,' *Research Management*, **20**, July, 1977, 34–42.

2 This method is discussed in J.W. Haefele, *Creativity and Innovation*, New York: Van Nostrand Reinhold, 1962, pp. 145–7; Sidney J. Parnes and Harold F. Harding (eds), *A Source Book for Creative Thinking*, New York: Charles Scribner's Sons, 1962, pp. 307–23; and Souder and Ziegler, 'A review of creativity and problem-solving techniques,' pp. 34–42.

3 Alex F. Osborn, *Applied Imagination*, New York: Scribner Book Companies, 1957, p. 138.

4 For a thorough discussion of the collective notebook method, see Haefele, *Creativity and Innovation*, p. 152.

Online sources

http://www.ericsson.com.
http://www.reuters.com/finance/stocks/companyProfile?symbol=ERIC.O.

3 Innovation and identifying and evaluating the opportunities

Scenario: Virgin Atlantic Airlines

In the early 1980s, Richard Branson was a well-renowned entrepreneur who founded Virgin Records. In 1984, he announced the launch of Virgin Atlantic Airways, an airline that focused on high quality and low cost. Virgin's inaugural flight to Newark was on 22 June 1984. The objective of the airline was: To provide the highest quality innovative service at excellent value for money for all classes of air travelers. By the late 1980s, over one million passengers had flown with Virgin Atlantic. Selling Virgin Records to Thorn EMI in 1992, Branson invested the proceeds in Virgin Atlantic. Creativity and innovation continued in the 1990s with the purchase of new planes, extending the route network, and generating greater creativity and innovation in all services to passengers. To establish a global partnership Branson sold a 49 percent stake in Virgin Atlantic to Singapore Airlines in 1999. Singapore Airlines paid £600.25 million for this stake, which included a capital injection of £49 million; Virgin Atlantic was valued at a minimum of £1.225 billion. The deal was finalized in early 2000 and Branson continues to hold a controlling 51 percent stake in Virgin Atlantic Airlines. However, in December 2012 Singapore Airlines sold their 49 percent stake to Delta Airlines for $360 million (£224 million).

Virgin Atlantic Airlines is well known for its innovations and competitiveness. It provides three classes of travel (Upper Class, Premium Economy and Economy); all classes offer in-flight entertainment. In March 2006, the new Virgin Clubhouse opened at Heathrow. This offered many unique features including a spa, hair salon, brasserie, cocktail bar and game room. Virgin Atlantic launched a new check-in facility at Heathrow Terminal Three in 2007. This provided Economy and Premium Economy passengers with a bright, more spacious and efficient check-in. Passengers traveling First Class had access to a private security corridor so they could proceed through the terminal to the Clubhouse.

At the time of writing, Virgin Atlantic has 38 aircraft that includes 13 Boeing 747s, six Airbus 340-300s and 19 Airbus A340-600s. A pioneering biofuel demonstration was held in 2008 with GE Aviation on a 747 between London and Amsterdam. This was the first ever commercial airline flight to use biofuel. The 787–9 Dreamliner is significantly more fuel efficient, burning approximately 27 percent less fuel per passenger compared to the A340-300, so Virgin Atlantic ordered 15 with the option to order an additional eight and purchasing rights on 20 more aircraft. Delivery of these planes continues from 2011 to the present.

Since its founding, Virgin Atlantic Airways has become the second largest British carrier serving major cities around the world. It has carried approximately 53 million passengers and has 9,000 employees worldwide. Virgin Atlantic is based at London's Heathrow and Gatwick and Manchester airports. In the United Kingdom, it is the second largest long-haul airline and the third largest European carrier over the North Atlantic, operating worldwide long-haul services to 30 destinations. Virgin Atlantic has led the way in the quality of service that competing airlines aim to follow.

Virgin Atlantic has achieved growth with its focus being to ensure that the service is customer driven with clear emphasis on providing good value, high quality and innovation. Branson's strong entrepreneurial mindset and fearless reputation, such as ballooning across the Atlantic Ocean, has provided Virgin with significant publicity. Additionally, James Bond films *Casino Royale* and *Quantum of Solace* featured the Virgin Atlantic aircraft resulting in major publicity worldwide. Branson's entrepreneurial attitude combined with the publicity gained has significantly contributed to the international success of the Virgin brand.

In addition to Virgin Atlantic Airlines, the Virgin Group has expanded beyond the airlines to include international 'Megastore' music retailing, book and software publishing, film- and video-editing facilities, clubs, trains, Virgin.com and financial advice companies resulting in more than 100 companies in 15 countries. Branson is a true entrepreneur and innovator. Besides all his business ventures, Branson is a trustee and supporter of a broad range of charities including the Virgin Healthcare Foundation. 'Change for Children Appeal' has raised over £2.75 million in support of worldwide children's healthcare initiatives. Branson is also engaged in the development of Charity Projects, which later was the basis for the very successful Charity Projects campaign.

With its successful history and leadership from a leading international entrepreneur who is willing to take risks and do what it takes to stay ahead, there is no doubt that Virgin Atlantic Airlines will continue to be creative and innovative and continuously identify and evaluate new opportunities.

Creativity

While creativity and innovation are frequently used interchangeably, there are fundamental distinctions between the two concepts. Creativity is a core building block for innovation. Creativity encompasses the process leading to the generation of new and valued ideas. Without creativity there would be no innovation because creativity is the foundation on which innovation emerges, develops and grows. Creativity is about developing ideas, processes or concepts, while innovation is the practical application of these. While not everyone can come up with ideas, creativity and innovation involves ideas, processes or concepts that are commercially viable. Creativity can lead to inventions but until they are commercialized they are not innovations. To be successful, the creativity and innovation must create new value for customers and generate return for the organization. Twitter was launched in March 2006 as an online social networking and micro blogging service that allows users to send and read 'tweets.' This innovative service has gained popularity among a broad population of celebrities and the general public with over 800 million users. Survival in a dynamic, competitive environment requires not mimicking and implementing the solutions and approaches of other organizations but developing new ideas and new ways of doing things. This requires that an organization utilizes their resources and the creative abilities of their people.

While it is the creativity in people and their ideas that produce innovations, organizations must support and nurture this for their benefit just like 3M allowing 15 percent and Google allowing 20 percent of staff time researching selected projects. Dyson and Salesforce.com focus on encouraging and following through on good ideas generated by individuals. The people involved in the creative and innovative process and the way they are organized and supported can have significant impact on the organization's innovation performance and its ability to be competitive through innovation.

Creativity is a critical skill for recognizing or creating opportunity in a dynamic environment. Creativity in products, services and processes is now more important than ever due to globalization and increased competitiveness. It is equally important in the established for-profit enterprise, the public sector organization and the new venture. Creativity and creative organizations are the success stories of the twenty-first century. A creative business like Virgin Atlantic Airlines that is willing to take risks and works on its mission and strategy to keep ahead of competition is the key to achieving competitive advantage in highly dynamic markets. Dawning Information Industry proved its creativity and innovation in October 2011 by building the world's fastest supercomputer that performed 2.57 quadrillion calculations per second. Dawning's technology has pushed the company's supercomputer market share past IBM's and HP's in China.

Creativity is the core of innovation and is necessary to develop innovative business concepts. It is fundamental to identify the patterns and trends that define an opportunity. While there are numerous perspectives including psychological, social, individual and organizational, creativity is the application of an individual's ability to identify and develop new ideas, processes or concepts in novel ways. It is the act of relating previously unrelated things in novel ways – a deviation from conventional perspectives. These ideas, processes or concepts must be useful and have value or meaning to become an innovation. Netflix is a highly creative company that recognized an opportunity and capitalized on the success of the DVD and the booming internet streaming service. The company was established in 1997 and since then has become a $9 billion powerhouse (outperforming Blockbusters). Netflix has been a most successful dot-com venture.

Creativity can range from low levels to relatively high levels. Lower-level creativity frequently involves incremental modifications and adjustments of an existing idea or a combination of two or more previously unrelated ideas in a noble and useful way. Higher-level creativity involves more breakthrough contributions. The level results in different forms of creativity:

- creativity that develops new ideas, processes or concepts
- creativity that modifies existing ideas, processes or concepts, for example:
  - a new, improved version that is more efficient and effective
  - additional features and functions added

    o   performs in a different setting
    o   targets a new audience
- creativity that combines things which were previously unrelated.

Whether creativity is entirely new, modified or a combination of previously unrelated things, it is a process of developing successful and useful ideas, processes or concepts. Creativity and innovation need people who are willing and eager to utilize their core competencies in the most creative and innovative ways. Being creative involves:

- being open minded and objective
- perseverance and dedication to continuously seek and produce ideas
- an ability to put existing or new ideas together in different ways
- drive and ability to overcome obstacles or find alternative solutions
- moderate risk taker
- intrinsic motivation
- internal locus of control
- desire to achieve and grow
- driven by growth and development.

Innovation

The link between innovation and creativity can be looked at in three stages. The first stage involves creativity through idea, activity and skill; the second stage involves invention through working model and prototype; and the final stage involves innovation through successful commercial introduction of the invention.

Creativity is a process of generating ideas and innovation and the refinement and implementation of those ideas. Creativity alone is not sufficient. Innovation is necessary to take the new or existing creative ideas and put them into action. It is the development, approval and implementation of new ideas, products, services or processes. Within the context of the organization, the focus is to bring a creative idea to fruition. From an organizational perspective, many great ideas never manifest beyond just that 'great idea.' Ideas that are brought to market must be acknowledged for their potential, have the necessary funding and the ability to overcome obstacles such as competitiveness, technological challenges and economic uncertainty. This is known as the innovation process; it is a fundamental process when referring to organizational creativity. Epocrates is a company that has created innovation by providing doctors and nurses with instant drug reference through a program for mobiles and laptops. With a click of a button the program allows medical professionals to make accurate prescribing decisions.

Creativity is initiated at the individual level. Individual creativity is related to factors such as personality, motivation, competency and expertise. At the organizational level, environmental factors such as culture and climate affect creativity and influence the behavior of individuals. The lack or insufficiency in creativity and innovation is one of the biggest threats to organizations today. Organizations such as Apple, American Greeting Cards, Google, 3M and Virgin Group practice creativity by looking broadly for ideas within their industries rather than where everyone else is looking. Future opportunities are typically about being able to differentiate from what everyone else is doing and linking creative ideas into innovations that are commercially viable and generate value.

Innovation successfully implements newness to any given situation. Innovation not only applies to the opening of new markets but also to new ways of serving established and matured segments. It can be the sequence of activities that introduces a new component into a social unit or a product or service. It can occur gradually with small incremental adjustments to current processes or products or happen explosively such as occurred with the internet, iPhone and social media. The innovation may not be entirely new or unfamiliar to the organization, but it should involve some identifiable change. Innovation can involve a political process that activates organizations to launch a significant new project for changing rules, regulations, procedures and structures related to the communication and exchange of information within the organization and with its external environment. While these projects may not require the invention of new technologies, they do require organizational change.

A key challenge for organizations is how to encourage and manage innovation. Innovation is perhaps the most pressing challenge facing organizations today. Essentially, innovation is the effort to create purposeful, focused change in the economic and social environment. Founders of innovative new ventures such as Herb Kelleher (Southwest Airlines),

Pierre Omidyar (eBay), Jeff Bezos (Amazon.com), Niklas Zennstrom (Skype), Michael Dell (Dell Computer) and Mark Zuckerberg (Facebook) are highly innovative entrepreneurs compared to entrepreneurs who establish less innovative ventures such as a McDonald's franchise, a Mercedes-Benz dealership, a newsstand or a consulting business.

The innovation process is more than creating a good idea. While the origin of an idea is important, and the role of creative thinking is fundamental to its development, innovation is a dynamic process involving both structural and social conditions. The sequence of steps in the innovation process typically starts with the awareness of a need and ends with the implementation of an innovation to satisfy the need. Rosabeth Moss Kanter, a Harvard Business School professor, outlines four major innovation tasks, which correspond roughly to the logic of the innovation process as it unfolds over time and to empirical data about the history of specific innovations.[1] These four tasks are:

1. Idea generation and activation of the drivers of the innovation.
2. Coalition building and acquisition of the power necessary to move the idea into reality.
3. Idea realization and innovation production, turning the idea into a model in order to use the product, plan or prototype.
4. Transfer or diffusion – the commercialization of the product and the final adoption of idea.

Some traits that facilitate innovation in an organization include:

- availability of resources for innovation and creativity
- open communication at all levels throughout the organization and among people with conflicting opinions
- decentralized structures that provide open access to innovation role models and coaches
- cohesive work groups with open, constructive, conflict resolution approaches that integrate and develop individual creativity
- low staff turnover
- personnel policies that reward and motivate innovative and creative behavior without fear of retribution for failure or too much success
- development of effective mechanisms to deal with environmental uncertainty and the ability to adapt to change.

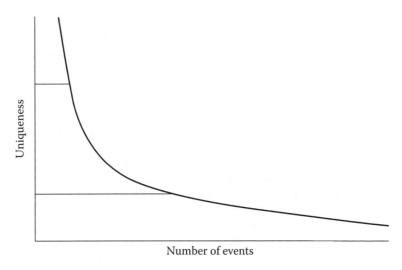

Figure 3.1   Innovation chart

The most successful organizations incorporate knowledge obtained from their past innovative experiences and successful new product launches.

Innovation is highly valued and necessary for the survival and growth of a technology venture. Innovation can take three basic forms, as indicated in Figure 3.1 – ordinary, technology and breakthrough. As indicated, the majority of innovations (the innovation with the highest incident rate) are ordinary innovations. These are innovations that have the smallest change in the way things are presently done or in the features of the product or service being offered. It may be just a simple, but better change in the way the product tastes or performs, or a change in the packaging or a new way of counting inventory.

The next infrequent type of innovation is the technological innovation. These are technological innovations that advance the process, product or service beyond what is presently available. These, where possible, are protected by a patent, trade secret (confidentiality agreements) or trademark that covers any intellectual property involved.

The smallest number of innovative events falls under the category of breakthrough innovations. These cause a radical transformation from the way things are presently done and can impact lifestyles of the

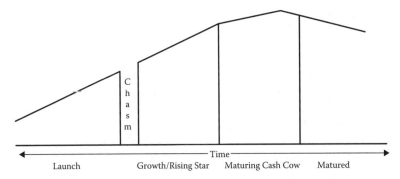

C
h
a
s
m

◄——————————————— Time ———————————————►
Launch   Growth/Rising Star   Maturing Cash Cow   Matured

Figure 3.2   Disruptive technologies

purchaser. These include such things as the personal computer, cell phone, internet, social networks and digital media. A technology company needs all these types of innovation constantly occurring so it can grow and prosper in its hypercompetitive, rapidly changing environment. Breakthrough innovations by successful companies are typically the subject of extensive intellectual property protection strategies.

The breakthrough innovation is often a disruptive technology causing a problem to occur in its launch and growth. A chasm frequently occurs between the initial launch and growth of the product in making sure that the product is not adapted by anyone other than the innovators, resulting in few if any sales occurring. This chasm must be bridged so that sales and profits can occur for the disruptive technology (Figure 3.2).

Design thinking

Design thinking is a new approach to create a breakthrough innovation and promote high-performance collaboration. It is quite different from analytical thinking and is a process for action. It is a method for discovering new opportunities and solving problems. While there are a variety of techniques and tools that can be used, the core process is somewhat universal.

It is generally understood that there are five key elements in design thinking: (1) defining the problem; (2) developing the options; (3) determining the direction; (4) selecting the best solution; and

(5) executing. The steps have some degree of similarity to those in the scientific process. Each of these steps are discussed in turn.

Defining the problem

This first step, correctly defining the problem, while sounding simple is often the most difficult part of design thinking. If the right problem is not defined, then of course the solution, if obtained, is for something else. Defining the problem is usually a team effort with a significant amount of participation by each team member.

Defining the problem involves observation – discerning what individuals actually do versus what they say they do. It also involves cross functional thinking in trying to find the real issues involved. Any preconceived notions or judgements need to be abandoned so that the right problem can be defined in such a way that creative solutions can occur. If the problem is a sitting apparatus, the problem is not to design a chair but to design something to suspend a person from the floor.

Developing the options

Once the problem is defined, the second element – developing the options – takes place. Care should be taken not to take the same approach as has been used in the past. Design thinking requires the creation of several solutions to the problem for consideration even when one solution seems obvious. For this to occur, multiple perspectives and team involvement are important. Involving multiple people develop a far richer range of solutions.

Determining the direction

The third stage – determining the direction – requires that the most promising solutions are carefully nurtured. An environment in an organization needs to be created such that each solution can be allowed to develop and grow. An environment of experimentation and testing allows the best solution to emerge. Often during this stage, ideas are combined to form an even better solution.

Selecting the best solution

From the many solutions maturing from the previous stage, the best solution needs to be selected. Prototypes of this solution are created and tested. This vigorous testing helps to ensure that the final solution is the best possible one.

Executing

Once the optimal form of the solution to the problem is found, the solution needs to be implemented. This execution element may prove difficult particularly when significant change is involved. Design thinking involves the acceptance of change and risk, which is often not easily embraced both by individuals and organizations. Execution also involves implementing design thinking on a continual basis as it is a repeatable process that will result in creative solutions to problems defined.

Opportunity analysis plan

The key to successful domestic and international venture creation is to develop an idea that solves a problem, satisfies a need for a large market or adds extensive value to the product, thereby increasing profit margins in a niche strategy. The ideas resulting need to be thought of in terms of satisfying a specific market need; as one corporate entrepreneur stated, 'Making the customer more profitable.'

What is deemed 'profitable' varies by the product or service idea – particularly whether the idea is in the business-to-business market or the business-to-consumer market. The uniqueness of the idea, its competitive advantage and the market size and characteristics can be determined through the development of an opportunity analysis (assessment). Opportunity analysis is often best accomplished by developing an opportunity analysis plan.[2] An opportunity analysis plan is a smaller version of a business plan. Compared to a business plan, it should:

- be shorter
- focus on the opportunity, not the venture
- have no financial plan, marketing plan or organizational plan
- be the basis on which to make the decision whether to act on an opportunity or wait until another, better opportunity comes along.

An opportunity analysis plan has four sections – two major sections and two minor sections. The first major section develops the product or service idea, analyses the competitive products and companies and identifies idea differentiation in terms of its unique selling propositions. This section includes:

- the market need for the product or service
- as complete a description as possible of the product or service
- the specific aspects of the product or service (as detailed as possible)
- the competitive products already available filling this need and features
- the companies in the product market space
- the unique selling propositions of the new product or service in light of the competition.

The second section of the opportunity analysis plan focuses on the market – its size, trends, characteristics and growth rate. It includes:

- the market need being filled
- the social condition underlining this market need
- any market research data available to describe this market need
- the size and characteristics of the domestic and/or international market
- the growth rate of the market.

The third section focuses on the corporate entrepreneur and the management team in terms of their skills and experience; it should include answers to the following questions:

- Why does this opportunity excite you? What will you keep you going when the business becomes difficult?
- How does the product or service idea fit into your background and experience?
- What business skills do you have to provide as equity capital?
- What business skills are needed?
- Where will you find these needed skills?

The final section of the opportunity analysis plan develops a timeline indicating the steps needed to successfully launch the venture and translate the idea into a viable business entity. This section should focus on:

- identifying each step
- determining the sequence of activities and putting these critical steps into some expected sequential order

- determining the time and money required at each step
- determining the total amount of time and money needed
- identifying the source of this needed money if not currently available.

Radical innovation

Corporate venturing plays a large part in igniting radical innovation in incumbent firms. Radical innovation transforms the relationship between customers and suppliers, restructures marketplace economics, displaces current products and often creates entirely new product categories. Radical innovation provides a platform for the long-term growth that corporate leaders desperately seek.[3] Hence, an effectively designed and managed internal corporate venture paves the way for radical innovation over incremental innovation by overtaking the organizational constraints.

Stage gate process

The stage gate process[4] developed by Robert C. Cooper, indicated in Figure 3.3, is an excellent approach for developing and evaluating new product/service ideas for launch. This process has also been called the product planning and development process, the product innovation process, the new product process, the gating system or the product launch system. The newer stages (creating and developing ideas; scoping; building business scenarios; development; testing and validation; launch; and post-launch review) represent important activities and actions that need to occur as the idea moves from its conception to its launch as a new product/service for the organization. Each stage has a prescribed set of actions that must take place. Most important are the gates that lead to a 'Go Forward' or 'Kill' product decision. Each gate has a common format:

1. required deliverables
2. criteria for judging the project
3. defined outputs that include an approved action plan for the next stage.

By using this process products/service can be stopped (eliminated) from the process so more resources can be devoted to product/service ideas that have a better chance of success for market introduction.

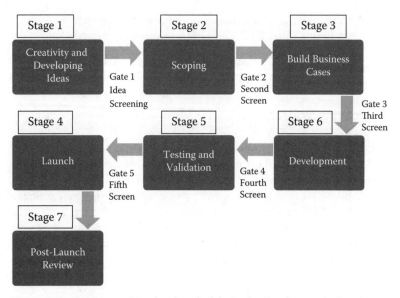

Note: Stage Gate® is a registered trademark of the Product Development Institute Inc.

Figure 3.3 Modified Stage Gate Process®

Summary

This chapter has focused on innovation and identifying and evaluating opportunities. First, the concepts of creativity and innovation are discussed. They include the three basic types of innovation and the barriers to each in an organization. Following a discussion of design technology, the chapter concludes by presenting the aspects of an opportunity analysis plan and the stage gate process.

NOTES

1 Rosabeth M. Kanter, 'When a thousand flowers bloom: Structural, collective, and social conditions for innovation in organizations,' *Research in Organizational Behavior*, **10**, 1988, 169–211.

2 For further reading about market opportunity analysis, see Stevens Robert, *Market Opportunity Analysis: Text and Cases*, London: Routledge, 2012, Chapter 7.

3 Richard Leifer, Christopher M. McDermott, Gina Coralleli O'Conner, Lois S. Peters, Mark P. Rice and Robert W. Veryzer, *Radical Innovation: How Mature Companies Can Outsmart Upstarts*, Boston, MA: Harvard Business School Press, 2000, p. 2.

4 Robert G. Cooper, *The Stage Gate® System: A Road Map from Idea to Launch – An Intro and Summary*.

Online sources

http://www.virgin-atlantic.com.

http://www.virgin.com.

http://www.bobcooper.ca/images/files/articles/2/1-The-Stage-Gate-System-A-
Roadmap-From-Idea-to-Launch.pdf.

4   Recognizing the opportunity for market disruption

*David W. Kralik**

Scenario: American Express

Of the 30 companies that compose the current Dow Jones Industrial Average, only three (Pfizer, Procter & Gamble and American Express) were founded prior to 1850. Of those, American Express stands out as being unique in its ability to respond to market dynamics and transform its business model over the decades of its existence.

American Express was founded in 1850 through a merger of three companies owned by Henry Wells (Wells & Company), William G. Fargo (Livingston, Fargo & Company) and John Warren Butterfield (Wells, Butterfield & Company).

Credit cards were non-existent in 1850 so many are surprised to learn that the company was initially formed to deliver express mail across country mostly by stagecoach. In 1855, the US Postal Service charged $0.03 for a letter weighing a half-ounce to travel cross-country up to 3,000 miles. By law, they could not carry parcels weighing more than four pounds at the beginning of the twentieth century. American Express and other companies recognized and offered services to fill that gap.

The company's entry into financial services began in 1882 when it launched a money order business to compete with the US Post Office. The immigration wave that hit the United States in the early twentieth century presented American Express with a new opportunity for market expansion. In 1905, the US Immigration Department awarded American Express with a contract to provide official currency exchange services after learning of fraud from independent moneychangers at Ellis Island.

In 1913, the company knew parcel post was not going to be in its future when President William Howard Taft signed legislation permitting the US Post Office to begin offering parcel post delivery because 'competition from a public entity was the only way to keep the express companies in check.'

As the company's official history notes, 'during the summer of 1914, approximately 150,000 American tourists were stranded when war engulfed Europe, many without access to funds. Banks had ceased to pay against foreign letters of credit or any other form of foreign paper.'

The company had already been a provider of Traveler's Cheques, an innovation they introduced in 1891, but in 1915, the outbreak of World War I presented an opportunity for the company to officially transform itself into a global travel concierge/travel service. That year, an executive at the company wrote a letter to the President justifying entry into this new market by noting:

> Already, we supply travelers with the tickets for their European tours; we receive and forward their mail; we provide reading and writing rooms for their convenience; we store and forward their baggage and packages; we engage their return steamship accommodations. In fact, we are doing already for travelers practically everything except that which is most remunerative to ourselves, namely, furnishing eastbound steamship tickets to Europe; providing hotel accommodations and conducting small parties desiring such a service.

In 1938, as the outbreak of World War II loomed, the company recognized this threat and 'mounted extensive preparations to protect its financial and real estate assets, including its principal offices in Berlin, London, Paris, Rome and Rotterdam.'

In the aftermath of World War II, a booming economy brought about another transformation of the company's business: the credit card. The concept of credit cards date to the 1920s but they were used in limited situations such as to buy gasoline or airline tickets from companies who accepted them. American Express had begun discussing introducing a charge card as early as 1946 but waited 12 years until it saw the success of Diner's Club and realized it could leverage its global network of relationships with banks and financial institutions to launch its own competing card.

Since the 1950s, the company has expanded and divested various businesses including investment banking, publishing and cable television, to name a few.

In the 2000s, after the introduction of the Centurion Card, American Express recognized that its brand was often associated with affluent customers and began making inroads to attract younger cardholders and to those who wanted a debit card option.

With the advent of companies like PayPal, Venmo, Square and products like ApplePay, the company is once again examining its business model with some executives openly saying that the credit card may cease to exist in the next 15 years. In 2011, the company formed American Express Ventures, a venture capital arm, to 'accelerate our efforts in digital commerce and financial inclusion.'

In the four years since its existence, American Express Ventures has made strategic investments into companies including Instacart, bill.com as well as software analytics providers like Radius & RetailNext.

Today, American Express describes itself as 'a global services company.' The company is careful not to pigeonhole itself into one market because it realizes from over 160 years of doing business that markets can dry up and new opportunities can present themselves overnight. As technology connects more people together, helps lower costs through economies of scale and changes how government and society operate, companies must be ready to respond. A successful business model yesterday may not be profitable in the future because of disruptive forces in the economy and society. Being able to identify new trends, and developing products and services to meet these trends, is key to a company's survival.

Overview of market disruption

By most accounts, Clayton Christensen first popularized the term 'disruptive innovation' in 1997 with his book, *The Innovator's Dilemma*. In his book, Christensen discusses forecasting demand for sustaining and disruptive technologies, the cycle of disruption and why companies are sometimes structurally unable to change and ultimately fail. While it is important to be able to identify and cultivate disruptive technologies,

RECOGNIZING THE OPPORTUNITY FOR MARKET DISRUPTION   45

it is also important to be able to identify when the opportunity is ripe for disruption.

The popularity of Christensen's book has also resulted in over-use of the term 'disruption' itself. In 2013, *The New Republic* noted that '*disruptive* is now slapped onto every act of cultural defiance or technical derring-do, whether it has to do with business or not.'[1] Around the same time, Max Nisen of *Business Insider* added that Silicon Valley 'killed disruption' because 'every time a company creates something new, beats another one out, or applies data or software to a new industry, it has instantly "disrupted."'[2] Writing in *The New Yorker*, author Jill Lepore described disruptive innovation as 'competitive strategy for an age seized by terror . . . in which fledgling companies use new technology to offer cheaper and inferior alternatives to products sold by established players.'[3]

If disruption is often thought of within a context of destruction, is it a good thing? The answer is, 'it depends.' Writing in *Harvard Business Review*, Greg Satell noted that 'successful disruption does not merely destroy, but creates a shift in mental models.'[4] Bad disruption can happen when entities enter a market and contribute nothing to increase the market's overall value. While we disagree with Lepore's assessment of disruption, she is correct when she noted that 'Disruption is a predictable pattern across many industries.'

Silicon Valley's extensive use of the term disruption might lead some to believe they invented the term. To the contrary, disruption is everywhere and has existed long before Christensen and Silicon Valley popularized the term.

Businesses face threats of new market entrants all the time and the result can be a loss of market share or even failure. At the core of every successful company is disruption; a new entrant found a way to attack an existing competitor by developing a new business model or a substitute solution. In that sense, market disruption is relatively simple.

Christensen's book is now almost 20 years old, written when Silicon Valley's impact on people's lives was in its infancy. What has not been sufficiently explored is whether there exist patterns to disruption that can help an entrepreneur or corporate strategist better identify and more easily recognize industries in need of change, and then build a strategy, with help from the examples in this chapter, to disrupt a market or industry. The industry examples in this chapter vary significantly: from air conditioners, digital music, finance, cars, food and the internet itself. These industries were chosen to help demonstrate that there is in fact a pattern to disruption and that trends can be identified to help business gain a competitive advantage.

Many times patterns of disruption overlap. Many of Richard Branson's companies – airlines, retailing and cola – were started in the face of entrenched competition. Branson found opportunities in markets that lacked transparency, had poor customer service, in which customers have been ripped off or under-served, where confusion reigns due to lack of standards and the competition is complacent.

Looking into past examples of market disruption, we have identified three broad indicators that foretell when a market is ripe for disruption: societal/macroeconomic indicators, political indicators and market ownership indicators.

Societal/macroeconomic indicators

A key to understanding market disruption is to know that markets are not efficient. Imperfect markets exist when demand of certain consumer classes cannot be met, when markets cannot react fast enough to changing demographics or when markets grow too fast and fail to create standards.

When markets fail to meet demand: consumer white spaces

Mark W. Johnson, co-founder of Innosight, a business consulting firm focused on disruptive innovation and strategic transformation, has described 'white space' as 'a metaphor about opportunity – a way to map your company's ability to address new opportunities or threats.' White spaces can exist wherever there is a gap between what a growing consumer class needs and the market offers.[5]

One such example is the growing segment of 'unbanked' or 'underbanked' individuals. In October of 2014, the Federal Deposit Insurance Corporation (FDIC), an independent US government agency that preserves and promotes public confidence in the US financial system, published the results of a survey about underbanked and unbanked individuals in the United States.

The FDIC found that 33 percent of the US population are either unbanked or underbanked.[6] The unbanked population has averaged around 8 percent since 2009 with the highest percentages found among non-Asian minorities, lower-income households, younger households and unemployed households. The FDIC defined unbanked as those who 'do not have an account at an insured institution' and underbanked as those who 'have an account, but have also obtained financial services and products from non-bank, alternative financial services (AFS) providers in the prior 12 months.'

The top reasons that households remained unbanked include lack of money (57 percent), dislike or mistrust of banks (34 percent) and account fees that are too high or unpredictable (30 percent) followed by privacy (26.4 percent).

Mitchell D. Weiss, an experienced financial services industry executive and adjunct professor of finance at the University of Hartford has said that the underbanked and unbanked 'are more likely to fall victim to the high-rate (predatory) side of the industry, like payday, account-advance, tax refund-advance and structured, settlement-advance loans, to name a few.'[7]

An entrepreneur armed with this knowledge, and experience in the banking industry, could look at ways to serve this demographic with financial products that offer lower, predictable fees, for example. Indeed, companies that have seized this opportunity have often used technology as the enabler of disruption and are broadly classified as being in the 'FinTech' or Financial Technology industry. CBInsights, a company that tracks funding for start-up companies, has found that funding for FinTech companies went from less than $1 billion in the second quarter of 2010 to nearly $3 billion in just the first three months of 2015. Collectively, the industry has raised over $13.7 billion.[8]

White spaces exist in both developed and emerging economies. Looking globally, perhaps one of the biggest gaps is the availability of affordable, clean housing. According to UN-Habitat, globally some 827 million people live in urban slums; by the year 2020, that number will be one billion.[9] In 2010, for example, South African President Jacob Zuma announced a new initiative to 'accommodate people whose salaries are too high to get government subsidies, but who earn too little to qualify for a normal bank mortgage.'[10] In South Africa, approximately 3.5 million (24 percent of the household population) are in this gap.

When markets react too slow to changing societal trends: the access economy

A second type of macroeconomic indicator is when markets fail or are slow to react to changing societal trends. In this particular instance, we are referring to the concept where 'consumers are paying to access someone else's goods or services for a particular period of time.'[11] Some have described this as the 'sharing' economy while others, including Giana M. Eckhardt and Fleura Bardhi, have stressed that 'when "sharing" is market-mediated – when a company is an intermediary between consumers who don't know each other – it is no longer sharing at all.'[12]

Regardless of the proper term, this trend started to gain acceptance in 1999 and has been fueled largely by the social nature of the internet. Writing in *Forbes*, author Steve Denning noted that

> [i]t created a generation of people who began doing something that cut to the heart of the way society has been organized for several hundred years. These people – mainly young – began *preferring* access to ownership. Instead of planning their lives on the premise of acquiring and owning more private property, this new generation began finding meaning and satisfaction in having access to things and interacting with other people in the process.[13]

Goldman Sachs Global Investment Research has found that 'It's not just homes: Millennials have been reluctant to buy items such as cars, music and luxury goods. Instead, they're turning to a new set of services that provide access to products without the burdens of ownership . . .'[14]

There is no specific date when the Access Economy emerged as a major force in the economy; like most trends, it built up over time. In 1999, the popularity of the music file-sharing site Napster was perhaps the first sign of its emergence. Jeremy Rifkin, the author of *The Zero Marginal Cost Society*, has noted that 'Napster changed the rules of the economic game. Many sellers and buyers disappeared, replaced by providers and users.'[15] Then, in 2006, after Facebook moved to an open registration policy, sharing photos and other digital content became more mainstream.

The Access Economy has also been fueled by economic reality. As Denning has suggested, 'as a result of the Great Stagnation of the world economy which disproportionately affects younger people. But the shift is also driven by a recognition that an economy of access and interaction could actually be better. It could be richer in meaning than anonymous commercial transactions.'[16]

The shift has been significant. Since 2008, over four million people have utilized a service called Airbnb, which allows users to rent out their home. Crunchbase, an online database that tracks start-ups, counts 23 competing companies that offer a similar business model to Airbnb.[17] In 2015, Barclays noted in an analyst report that Airbnb had already overtaken the largest hotel companies. Airbnb has an estimated one million rooms for rent compared to the largest hotel company in the world, Intercontinental Group, which has a portfolio of 687,000 rooms.[18]

Today, society has shifted to an acceptance where nearly every consumable good owned by someone can be rented out during idle use. In 2014, PriceWaterhouseCoopers estimated that total revenues for the five most prominent sharing economy sectors – peer-to-peer (P2P) finance, online staffing, P2P accommodation, car sharing and music/video streaming – could hit $335 billion by 2025, up from just $15 billion today.[19]

An entrepreneur interested in this space might look at other products they own and explore whether a market exists to rent them out to willing users. Writing in *Fast Company* magazine, Danielle Sacks has suggested that new products within the Access Economy fit the criteria, 'cost more than $100 but less than $500, easily transportable, and infrequently used.'[20]

When markets grow too fast and fail to create standards: iTunes

As a result of all the illegal music downloading, the original, free, peer-to-peer file-sharing site Napster was shut down in 2001 after a series of lawsuits brought by the music industry. But, in the absence of Napster, other sites like Kazaa appeared and the piracy continued.

In 2003, sales of digital music were relatively new, but growing quickly. The Recording Industry Association of America (RIAA) estimated that just 1.3 percent of all music sales were digital in 2003; two years later, that number was 5.7 percent.[21] Industries that enjoy rapid sales growth like this often experience challenges to scalability because standards are lacking. The proliferation of Napster-like clones such as Kazaa created an environment where product quality and downloads were unreliable. As Ed Nash wrote in the *Wall Street Journal*, 'The genie would not go back into the bottle. The lawsuits were costly and cumbersome, the music industry wasn't coming up with a viable solution.'[22]

In 2003, Steve Jobs, Chief Eexecutive Officer (CEO) of Apple Inc., recognized a problem; sites like Napster proliferated because, Jobs said, there was no reliable alternative.[23] As Jobs noted to his biographer, Walter Isaacson, 'if the music companies had been able to agree on a standardized encoding method for protecting music files, then multiple online stores could have proliferated.'[24]

On April 28 2003, Jobs stood before a packed audience ready to offer a product that, he felt, would bring music piracy under control. The iTunes music store was a new product but, more importantly, it was a new standard. To compete, Apple struck deals with the five largest music labels at the time (Warner, Universal, Sony, BMG and EMI). In doing so, it offered a viable solution: consistent quality, reliable downloading, no monthly subscription fees and all songs would be priced at a transparent $0.99 each. In 2014, iTunes still accounted for 52 percent of all music downloads.[25] While Apple's market share in digital music downloads is now decreasing as a result of a shift in consumer preference to streaming music amidst the growth of the Access Economy, it is still important to note that Apple was successful in disrupting the digital music industry by not only offering a new product but a new standard, a platform, that didn't exist.

Trends brought about by changes in public policy

Understanding market disruption also requires an appreciation for how the legal and regulatory environment impacts trends. Government, whether through direct involvement or lack thereof, and the speed at which they react, can have a significant impact on industry. Government, at all levels, have a variety of tools including laws, regulations, executive orders and even court decisions that, some argue, give the perception of 'picking winners and losers' in the free market.

The increased size and complexity of government requires entrepreneurs to be more mindful of how government can create opportunities. However, this is not a new phenomenon.

BOX 4.1   WHERE TO LOOK FOR TRENDS

There are a number of places a seasoned market researcher can help you find the next trends. The first place is seeing what data is out there and whether there is a noticeable increase or decrease. The US government collects data through a variety of agencies and bureaus (that is, Bureau of Labor Statistics, Bureau of Energy Statistics) as well as through the Census Bureau. Other sources of data are actual market research agencies like Forrester, Gallup and Gartner. Finally, sites like eBay, Google and Amazon all have dedicated research teams that help analyze all the user-generated data on their sites. For example, eBay, with 100 million users and 400 million active listings, has an economics team that looks at such issues as trust, reputation, marketing effectiveness and pricing strategies. Amazon, with $88 billion in net sales in 2014 and over five billion items sold in 2014,[26] offers the public a way to see what is in demand now, filtered by category. Finally, Google with a 67 percent share of the search engine market[27] offers Google Trends as a powerful tool to understand what people are searching for by topic, region and whether it is affected by seasonality.

Trends for a 65 million strong demographic

In the United States, the US Census Bureau estimates that 65 million people were born between the years 1946–64.[28] The Baby Boom has and will continue to have a profound effect on consumption and consumer behavior. Demand for new products, especially those focused on catering to an aging population, will continue to increase for at least the next 30 years. Wealth management and healthcare services, including assisted living, are excellent trends that can be mined for new business opportunities.

Today, the youngest of the Baby Boomers is 51 years old. The coming Baby Boom retirement will also have a profound effect on how the US federal government operates. According to the US federal government's Office of Personnel Management, by the year 2016, 60.8 percent of the government non-seasonal full-time permanent workforce will be eligible to retire.[29] Some have suggested that the upcoming mass retirement of civil service workers might provide an opportunity for government to outsource additional services instead of relying on insourced talent.

Ken Chenault, CEO and Chairman of American Express, has often shared how government policy necessitated a change in the company's business model. American Express was founded in 1850 as a service to transport packages across the United States by stagecoach. But, in 1912, President William Taft signed legislation that allowed the US Post Office to begin parcel post delivery. In 2013, the US Inspector General released a report on the 100th anniversary of parcel post delivery and summarized the political landscape by noting:

> The principal argument was that competition from a public entity was the only way to keep the express companies in check. With the express companies largely discredited in the public's mind, all political parties supported Parcel Post legislation in the election of 1912, and it became effective on January 1, 1913. Parcel Post was an immediate hit with the public and businesses; more than 4 million packages were shipped on the first day. Parcel Post transformed the commercial marketplace, as companies like Sears, Roebuck and Montgomery Ward blanketed the country with mass produced goods that raised the national standard of living.[30]

As a result of this, American Express knew that parcel delivery was not going to be in their future. So, it developed the Traveler's Cheque and transformed into a global travel concierge/travel service.[31] Many of today's companies could learn from the success that American Express has had in transforming its business as a result of government intervention in the free market. An entrepreneur who carefully monitors government involvement in their industry can stand to benefit if they can position their product as a solution prior to any impending change in the legal or regulatory environment.

Government can disrupt markets not only through direct entry (as in the case of parcel post) but also by making products illegal. In 1987, 46 countries signed the Montreal Protocol that established requirements for phasing out ozone-depleting CFC gases, including R-22 refrigerant. The treaty, which has undergone several amendments, set a deadline for the year 2020 where 'chemical manufacturers will no longer be able to produce R-22 to service existing air conditioners and heat pumps.'[32] R-22 gas had been used for over 40 years and, while its phase-out was not immediate, an entrepreneur with experience in this industry could position a new company to take advantage of this opportunity by introducing new products to address the ban including of products that use a replacement gas or offering services to retro-fit existing systems.

Another example of government involvement that can affect trends is through regulation and reclassification. In 1990, the US Congress passed the Organic Foods Production Act that, for the first time, established a set of rules for what foods can be classified as 'organic.'[33] Similar to the situation with digital music and iTunes, there was confusion over multiple standards. In 2002, after a 12-year process, the new rules took effect and Michael F. Jacobson, Executive Director of the Center for Science in the Public Interest, an advocacy group pushing for the classification, said, 'The law, for the first time, will assure consumers that foods that purport to be organic, really are. That increased consumer confidence should lead to greatly increased consumption of organic foods – and a bright outlook for growers, processors, and marketers of those foods.'[34] Jacobson was correct. In 1990 the United States Department of Agriculture (USDA) reported that sales of organic fruits and vegetables were less than $250 million per year. Ten years later, sales were $2.2 billion.[35]

One company that successfully rode this trend was Whole Foods Market, which was founded in 1980 in Austin, Texas. In January of 1990, with only eight stores (including their first outside Texas) the company launched a private label called 'Whole Foods' utilizing suppliers that were committed to producing quality organic products.[36] In 1992, the company went public at a price of $2.12 per share with a market cap of $104 million.[37] Today, the company has a market cap in excess of $10 billion with $14 billion in sales from 430 stores and plans to expand to 1,200 stores globally.[38]

Companies like Whole Foods often take a reactionary approach to new government policies by developing new strategies and products to comply with new rules and regulations. But another, more aggressive, strategy is to lobby for changes in rules that create a more level playing field between existing companies and start-up ventures. Tesla Motors is one such example.

Founded in 2003 by Elon Musk, the company has, with some success, fought government policy to allow direct-to-consumer sales of its automobiles. There efforts have earned the ire of the National Automobile Dealers Association (NADA), a trade association that favors existing laws in 48 states that forbid or restrict the ability of automakers to sell vehicles directly to the public. According to Tesla, 'Automotive franchise laws were put in place decades ago to prevent a manufacturer from unfairly opening stores in direct competition with an *existing franchise dealer* that had already invested time, money and effort to open and promote their business.'[39]

In the US, Tesla operates over 90 show rooms that educate the public about its all-electric cars.[40] While no sales are conducted in these show rooms, some view these show rooms as an end-run around the decades-old franchise law.[41] In October of 2012, Musk released a statement on Tesla's website, 'The U.S. automotive industry has been selling cars the same way for over 100 years and there are many laws in place to govern exactly how that is to be accomplished. We do not seek to change those rules.'[42]

Yet, Tesla has taken a very aggressive lobbying approach to level the playing field. In 2013, the company lost legislative efforts in Texas (which declined to make an exception to existing auto dealer rules) and North Carolina (which approved a bill making it illegal to sell new cars over the internet).[43] In February of 2015, the company lobbied the Arizona legislature to pass legislation that would allow the company to bypass the existing auto dealer sales model and sell its cars directly to the public if the company establishes a service center in the state.[44]

Tesla has also been able to use existing government laws to earn revenue from new products. In 2015, Tesla announced that it was entering the energy storage market with a new product called the Powerwall. According to the company's website, Powerwall is 'a home battery that charges using electricity generated from solar panels, or when utility rates are low, and powers your home in the evening. It also fortifies your home against power outages by providing a backup electricity supply. Automated, compact and simple to install, Powerwall offers independence from the utility grid and the security of an emergency backup.' For a company like Tesla, already a pioneer in electric batteries for cars, Powerwall was a relatively easy product line extension. But there may have been another reason for Tesla to enter this market.

In April of 2015, Bloomberg reported that Tesla 'is on track to reap as much as $65 million in [California] SGIP [Self Generation Incentive Program] rebates, which are designed to encourage investment in alternative energy.'[45] According to the Center for Sustainable Energy, the state of California's SGIP 'was initially conceived as a peak-load reduction program in response to the California energy crisis of 2000–2001, in which Californians experienced electrical outages throughout the state.'[46] For companies looking to break into the program it has a budget of $83 million and covers as much as 60 percent of a project's costs.[47]

Market share ownership indicators

Start-up ventures can also find success by looking at market share ownership indicators.

Opportunities exist where a market share is concentrated with a few companies and where no one company has a significant share of the market. There are two generally accepted ways that market share can be calculated to determine whether an industry exhibits high, medium or low concentration.

The first, called CR4 concentration ratio, is a simple method that adds the market share percentages of the four largest firms in the industry.[48] Concentration ratios range from 0 to 100 percent. An industry with a ratio between 0–50 percent is considered low concentration; an industry with a ratio between 50–80 percent is considered an oligarchy; industries with a ratio between 80–100 percent are either an oligarchy or monopoly.

Because the CR4 method only accounts for the top four (or sometimes eight) firms, and does not account for distribution of the firm size, the resulting data may not provide a thorough analysis of market concentration when compared to a second method, the Herfindahl–Hirschman Index (HHI).

The HHI calculates market concentration by adding the sum of the squares of the market shares of the 50 largest firms. For example, if two firms each have a 35 percent share of the market, then the HHI would be $35^2 + 35^2 = 2450$. The HHI has been used by the US Department of Justice (DOJ) as one means to evaluate market competitiveness in the event of a horizontal merger. The DOJ classifies unconcentrated markets as those with an HHI below 1500; moderately concentrated markets are those with an HHI between 1500 and 2500; highly concentrated markets are those with an HHI above 2500.

A corporate strategist looking to advise management on where their next acquisition should occur might calculate the HHI of an industry in order to gauge if the industry could withstand a new entrant.

Additionally, a market entry strategy would vary in industries with a low HHI (many small firms) verses an industry with a high HHI (few large firms).

It is entirely possible that the HHI was a factor in Procter & Gamble's (P&G) decision eight years ago to enter the dry cleaning services business. According to a market research report by IBISWorld, the dry cleaning industry has over 36,000 businesses and 'a very low level of market share concentration.' In 2015, the top four dry cleaning companies, all of which are national franchisors, represent less than 3 percent of total industry revenue and 80 percent of all establishments have five or fewer employees.[49]

As noted previously, disruption can be both a positive or negative force to an industry and existing businesses. IBISWorld also notes that dry cleaning is currently experiencing negative growth and will continue to see negative growth, contracting 1.2 percent every year through 2020. The main reasons for the decline are 'Falling demand for dry cleaning services, unfavorable shifts in consumer preferences and increasing competition from coin-operated Laundromats.' Additionally, as more businesses adopt a casual dress code, demand for professional cleaning services has dropped.

Given that the overall industry is experiencing a slight decline, it is not surprising that customer service and innovation are lacking in this otherwise stagnant industry. Jeff Wampler, CEO of P&G's subsidiary that runs Tide Dry Cleaners, has said, 'Consumers have generally been dissatisfied with dry cleaning . . . There has been poor customer service, missing buttons, an unpleasant smell.'[50]

In situations where industries are experiencing negative or even stagnant growth, new entrants can be successful by offering a better customer service experience, especially through technology innovation and this appears to be Tide's strategy.

In August of 2015, a press release from Tide emphasized their desire to be more customer-friendly and offer new innovations. 'The Tide Dry Cleaners system includes the convenience of drive-thru concierge services and 24-hour pick-up and drop-off with Tide Dry Cleaners Anytime[SM] kiosk and drop-box. Through its partnership with GreenEarth® and utilization of Tide fabric care, Tide Dry Cleaners offers cleaning technology to care for a range of garments and textiles.'[51]

As Jim Gallagher of the *St. Louis Post-Dispatch* noted, 'the manufacturing company hopes to leverage the fame of its Tide laundry detergent into a foothold in the service economy.'[52] Andrew Martin of the
International Herald Tribune added, 'where other dry cleaning entrepreneurs have tried to come up with clever business models for dry
cleaning, Procter & Gamble's primary innovation is in the brand name
itself: Tide Dry Cleaners.'[53]

P&G's decision to enter the dry cleaning services market was led
by FutureWorks, its global 'entrepreneurial engine.' In 2010, the
New York Times noted that FutureWorks was looking for franchise
opportunities in industries where 'ownership was fragmented and
consumers weren't satisfied. It came up with a three-inch binder of
ideas.'[54]

Because market concentration is low in the dry cleaning industry, and
no major players exist, a new entrant can also be successful by adopting a strategy of 'nationalizing an industry,' which can result in a more
uniform, consistent product and possibly lower costs by leveraging
economies of scale.

For over 65 years, P&G has been a leader in fabric care, selling a variety
of soaps and detergents including Tide to clean clothes. P&G is clearly
the market leader for laundry detergent in North America; in 2013 the
Wall Street Journal noted that annual sales on its detergent products
exceeded $4.5 billion.[55]

P&G's entry into this market with near-limitless funds doesn't necessarily guarantee success. On 28 August 2015, after eight years, P&G
opened their 30th Tide Dry Cleaner store in North America, located in
Draper, Utah.[56] It remains to be seen whether P&G can 'nationalize the
dry cleaning industry' with their approach but all signs suggest they are
taking a cautious approach if you look at past attempts.

In 1998, Unilever invested in a company called Zoots with a goal to
revolutionize the dry cleaning industry. According to the *Boston Globe*,
'Zoots was one of the country's biggest chains, with about 75 stores
and roughly 115 delivery routes across eight states, serving more than
300,000 customers.'[57]

However, by 2008, investors had lost $150 million and the company's
franchise locations were sold off. One of the major assumptions that

proved to be incorrect was that this industry could be franchised. However, according to the *Boston Globe*, 'Unlike fast-food chains that standardize all the food and cooking techniques, dry cleaners deal with thousands of different garments with unique issues on a daily basis.'[58] According to company insiders, Zoots was spending 6 percent of its revenue on loss prevention, paying out claims for lost or damaged garments, which is about six times the industry average. Additionally, a shrinking industry, tightening credit card and the departure of the company's senior leadership, who were responsible for the early vision, were also to blame. Around the same time as Zoots' failure, National Dry Cleaners filed for bankruptcy protection and in 2010 US Dry Cleaning Corporation did the same.

As seen in the example of Tide Dry Cleaners, taking an 'industry nationalization' approach to market disruption requires not only carefully studying the industry to ensure that it can benefit from economies of scale but also learning from failed efforts to avoid making the same mistakes twice.

Whereas P&G had the benefit of years of planning and the ability to learn from the past, in 1995, Pierre Omidyar had no such advantage when he started eBay. In his founder's letter, Omidyar referred to eBay as 'a grand experiment in Internet commerce.'[59] Always fascinated with markets, Omidyar believed in the theory that 'in financial markets, goods will trade at a fair value only when everyone has access to the same information.'[60]

A software developer by trade, Omidyar recognized the potential of the internet to break down information silos and connect people to freely share this information. In 2005, he was interviewed by *BusinessWeek* and said, 'We have technology, finally, that for the first time in human history allows people to really maintain rich connections with much larger numbers of people. Everywhere, people are getting together and connecting. And using the Internet, they're disrupting whatever activities they're involved in.'[61]

But one of the biggest issues that eBay had to address early on was trust. As Omidyar noted in his speech to the Academy of Achievement, 'And so with eBay, the whole idea there was just to help people do business with one another on the Internet. And people thought it was impossible because how could people on the Internet – remember this is 1995 – how could they trust each other?'[62]

To solve this problem, Omidyar decided to launch a second experiment, the feedback forum. In launching the feedback forum, Omidyar noted, 'I hope to make it easier to conduct business with strangers over the net . . . Use our feedback forum. Give praise where it is due; make complaints where appropriate.'[63]

Years later, Omidyar acknowledged that '[The feedback forum] was a real experiment, and I didn't know what to expect.'[64] But it proved to be one of the most consequential decisions that helped the company grow by discouraging fraud. It served as 'as a self-regulating mechanism that encourages good behavior and high morals.'[65] In a press release, the company added, 'at the core of the eBay community is the Feedback Forum, where registered buyers and sellers build up their online trading reputation. The Feedback Forum provides users with the ability to comment on their experiences with another individual.'[66]

Omidyar was one of the early pioneers of the internet to recognize that technology can introduce economies of scale and be an enabling force for disrupting industries that have survived by being inefficient. As Omidyar noted in 2000 in a speech in London to the Academy of Achievement, 'What eBay did really was to create a new market, one that wasn't really there before. And that was a global market for the kind of goods that were usually traded at flea markets and garage sales.'[67]

In effect, eBay used technology to nationalize the garage sale industry and its success inspired others to recognize that the same could be done in other industries. As John Bladon and Paul Daugherty noted in *Electric Light & Power*, 'But what eBay has done to centralize a million neighborhood garage sales, for example, merely represents the powerful opportunity e-commerce provides to any organization that possesses imagination, speed and flexibility.'[68]

There are, however, some who disagree with the notion that the internet can build an efficient market. Omidyar has often spoken about one of the decisions to start eBay that came from the reality of buying a stock at its IPO price. Omidyar wanted to invest in an IPO of a gaming company that went public for $15 a share. Unfortunately, his broker ended up buying the stock at $24 a share because '$15 was the ideal price, not the price that people like [Omidyar] can get . . . the theory of efficient markets is really great – in theory. In practice, regular people are locked out.'[69]

Writing in *Computerworld* back in 1999, David Moschella argued that 'one of the basic principles of modern economics is that the intrinsic value of a product has almost nothing to do with its price . . . Online auctions can augment this reality, but they can't change it. From an economic perspective, auctions will prove most suited to those cases where there's a clear, but typically temporary, market imbalance.'[70]

In an on-air commentary for Canadian TV back in 1999, Deidre McMurdy echoed these comments and went on to suggest that eBay may have killed the entire concept of garage sale bargain hunting. He noted, 'But with the Internet there are now potentially millions of bidders in the mix with minimal transaction costs. And that drives up prices. It's pretty perfect for vendors but bargains depend on market imperfections: things like inadequate information, barriers of time or distance – none of which exist on the 'Net.'[71]

McMurdy's comment raises an important issue regarding the disruptive effect of eBay: has it been destructive or constructive? In 2006, ACNielsen and eBay surveyed eBay sellers and concluded that 'approximately 1.3 million sellers around the world use eBay as their primary or secondary source of income.'[72]

In 1998, Mark Albright of the *St. Petersburg Times* opined that 'e-commerce forces eBay and Craigslist . . . are attracting more bargain-hunting consumers, contributing to a sharp drop in flea market sales in Florida the past decade.[73] Albright went on to compare gross sales of Florida-based flea markets from 1997 through 2008 and suggested that the sharp drop from $212 million in 1998 to just $139 million in 2007 could be attributed to online sites like eBay.

But in 2010, the *Daily News of Los Angles* noted that 'With online sites such as eBay and Craigslist leading the way, entrepreneurs, thrift stores and national chains are battling over the growing market for used goods. Small boutiques offer secondhand clothes. Even Best Buy is getting into the resale act, announcing that it will start selling used video games later this summer.'[74]

The example of eBay is also important to note how companies can themselves be up-ended by the very means that made them disruptive in the first place. In 2012, eBay's Chief Finance Officer Bob Swan participated in the Piper Jaffray consumer conference and stated that the e-commerce industry, which eBay helped launch, was at 'an inflection point.'[75] Specifically, Swan noted that

> in a relatively short period of time, shopping is no longer about going to the mall or being tethered behind your computer at your desk. It's now being influenced dramatically by mobile and the innovations that the industry is developing, available for the consumers in the palm of their hand.

When eBay was founded in September of 1995, it was initially known as AuctionWeb, which reflected its primary source of revenue: items being sold at auction. In the conference call, Swan noted that in 2008, eBay's revenue was evenly split between the traditional auction and what they referred to as 'fixed price.' By 2012, auction sales had shrunk to a little over 30 percent of the business in favor of fixed price. As Swan noted, 'A fixed price format, which is more for the convenience-oriented shopper, which is roughly 65% of our business, and growing in the mid- to upper-teens.'

Today, Omidyar's grand experiment has 31,500 employees and $14 billion in annual revenue. In an interview with the *New York Times'* David Carr, Omidyar said, 'Technologists come at a problem from the point of view that the system is working a certain way and if I engage in that system and actually change the rules of the system, I can make it work a different way. If you think about what did Google do, what did Facebook do, what did Twitter do, what did eBay do, they all created systems that changed the way the world works at a very large scale.'[76]

Summary

In 2013, an article in *The New Republic* said that 'disruptive is now slapped onto every act of cultural defiance or technical derring-do, whether it has to do with business or not.'[77] There was disruption fatigue with Silicon Valley being the most recent abuser of the term to describe every highly-ambitious new start-up. In truth, though, behind every successful venture there has always been a story about disruption; how they disrupted a market, an entrenched competitor or developed an entirely new business model or replacement solution to an existing problem. If disruption is constantly occurring, does it occur in a pattern? Using examples across six diverse industries (from air conditioners, digital music, finance, cars, food and the internet itself), the chapter discusses societal, macroeconomic, political and market ownership indicators that can predict when a market is ripe for disruption. In addition, the trends identified can collectively help any entrepreneur or corporate strategist to better identify and more easily recognize industries in need of change.

NOTES

* David W. Kralik is a Business Formation Advisor and Strategist with a global mindset. Using the lean startup methodology, he has advised dozens of award-winning companies. Prior to earning his MBA from the Thunderbird School of Global Management, he held various positions in politics, including Head of Strategy for former Speaker Newton 'Newt' Gingrich. His work has been profiled in the *Washington Post* and *Investor's Business Daily*. His work has also transcended pop culture, having been featured in a song by a platinum-award-winning musician, on an episode of *The Simpsons* and in *Playboy* magazine. In his spare time, he plays the saxophone and enjoys global travel, having travelled to all seven continents.

1 Judith Shulevitz, 'Don't you dare say "disruptive",' *The New Republic*, 16 August, 2013. http://www.newrepublic.com/article/114125/disruption-silicon-valleys-worst-buzzword.

2 Max Nisen, 'How "disrupt" got turned into an overused buzzword,' *Business Insider*, 28 September, 2013. http://www.businessinsider.com/how-silicon-valley-killed-disruption-2013-9#ixzz3at FyRpLw.

3 Jill Lepore, 'The disruption machine,' *The New Yorker*, 23 June, 2014. http://www.newyorker.com/magazine/2014/06/23/the-disruption-machine?currentPage=all.

4 Greg Satell, 'Let's stop arguing about whether disruption is good or bad,' *Harvard Business Review*, 21 May, 2015. https://hbr.org/2015/05/lets-stop-arguing-about-whether-disruption-is-good-or-bad.

5 Mark W. Johnson, 'Where is your white space?,' *Harvard Business Review*, 12 February, 2010. https://hbr.org/2010/02/where-is-your-white-space.

6 Susan Burhouse, Karyen Chu, Ryan Goodstein et al., *2013 FDIC National Survey of Unbanked and Underbanked Households*, Washington, DC: Federal Deposit Insurance Corporation. https://www.fdic.gov/householdsurvey/2013report.pdf.

7 Michael Estrin, '6 reasons to be unbanked or underbanked,' *Bankrate*. http://www.bankrate.com/finance/banking/reasons-unbanked-underbanked-1.aspx#ixzz3pbvcHZeQ.

8 https://www.cbinsights.com/blog/category/industry/fin-tech-industry/.

9 Scott Anderson, *The BIG IDEA Global Spread of Affordable Housing*, Arlington, VA: NextBillion and Ashoka Full Economic Citizenship, 2012, p. 12.

10 President Jacob Zuma, 'State of the nation address by his excellency JG Zuma, President of the Republic of South Africa; joint sitting of parliament, Cape Town,' 11 February, 2010. http://www.thepresidency.gov.za/pebble.asp?relid=211.

11 Giana M. Eckhardt and Fleura Bardhi, 'The sharing economy isn't about sharing at all,' *Harvard Business Review*, 28 January, 2015.

12 Ibid.

13 Steve Denning, 'Three strategies for managing the economy of access,' *Forbes*, 2 May, 2014. http://www.forbes.com/sites/stevedenning/2014/05/02/economic-game-change-from-ownership-to-access/.

14 'Millennials coming of age,' *Goldman Sachs*. http://www.goldmansachs.com/our-thinking/pages/millennials/.

15 Jeremy Rifkin, 'The zero marginal cost society,' *St. Martin's Griffin*, July, 2015, p. 185.

16 Denning, 'Three strategies for managing the economy of access.'

17 'Airbnb,' *CrunchBase*. https://www.crunchbase.com/organization/airbnb/competitors.

18 Michael B. Baker, 'Barclays: Airbnb usage to surpass hotel cos., but not for business travel,' *Business Travel News*, 16 January, 2015. http://www.businesstravelnews.com/Hotel-News/ Barclays--Airbnb-Usage-To-Surpass-Hotel-Cos-But-Not-For-Business-Travel/?ida=Hotel%20 Chains&ta-mgmt.

19 Gill Carson, 'Five key sharing economy sectors could generate £9 billion of UK revenues by 2025,' *PWC*, 15 August, 2014. http://pwc.blogs.com/press_room/2014/08/five-key-sharing-economy-sectors-could-generate-9-billion-of-uk-revenues-by-2025.html.

20 Danielle Sacks, 'The sharing economy,' *Fast Company*, 18 April, 2011. http://www.fastcompany.com/1747551/sharing-economy.

21 '2008 Consumer Profile,' Recording Industry Association of America.

22 Ed Nash, 'How Steve Jobs saved the music industry,' *Wall Street Journal*, 21 October, 2011. http://www.wsj.com/articles/SB10001424052970204002304576629463753783594.

23 Walter Isaacson, *Steve Jobs*, New York: Simon & Schuster, 2011, p. 395.

24 Ibid.

25 Russ Crupnick, 'One third of US consumers still buy music downloads, even as streaming gains momentum,' *MusicWatch*, 9 April, 2015. http://www.musicwatchinc.com/blog/one-third-of-us-consumers-still-buy-music-downloads-even-as-streaming-gains-momentum/.

26 Ainsley O'Connell, 'Amazon sold 5 billion items in 2014,' *Fast Company*, 1 June, 2015. http://www.fastcompany.com/3040445/fast-feed/amazon-sold-5-billion-items-in-2014.

27 Ashley Zeckman, 'Google search engine market share nears 68%,' *Search Engine Watch*, 20 May, 2014. http://searchenginewatch.com/sew/study/2345837/google-search-engine-market-share-nears-68.

28 Kelvin Pollard and Paola Scommegna, 'Just how many baby boomers are there?,' *Population Reference Bureau*, April, 2014. http://www.prb.org/Publications/Articles/2002/JustHowManyBabyBoomersAreThere.aspx.

29 *An Analysis of Federal Employee Retirement Data*, Washington, DC: US Office of Personnel Management, March, 2008.

30 Office of Inspector General United States Postal Service, '100 years of parcel post,' 20 December, 2013, Report Number: RARC-WP-14-004. https://www.uspsoig.gov/sites/default/files/document-library-files/2015/rarc-wp-14-004_0.pdf.

31 Devin Leonard and Elizabeth Dexheimer, 'How bad will it get for American Express?,' *Bloomberg*, 15 October, 2015. http://www.bloomberg.com/features/2015-how-amex-lost-costco/.

32 'Ozone layer protection,' *United States Environmental Protection Agency*. http://www3.epa.gov/ozone/title6/phaseout/22phaseout.html.

33 'Organic foods production act of 1990,' *United States Department of Agriculture*, 16 November, 2005. http://www.ams.usda.gov/sites/default/files/media/Organic%20Foods%20Production%20Act%20of%201990%20(OFPA).pdf.

34 'Hallelujah! Organic labeling rules take effect,' *Center for Science in the Public Interest*, 17 October, 2002. http://cspinet.org/new/200210171.html.

35 Carolyn Dimitri and Catherine Greene, 'Recent growth patterns in the U.S. organic foods market,' *Economic Research Service/USDA*. http://www.ers.usda.gov/media/255736/aib777c_1_.pdf.

36 'History of Whole Foods Market, Inc.,' *Funding Universe*. http://www.fundinguniverse.com/company-histories/whole-foods-market-inc-history/.

37 'History and timeline,' *Whole Foods Market*. http://media.wholefoodsmarket.com/history/.

38 Jeff Morganteen, 'Whole foods CEOs: we want 1,200 stores in US,' CNBC, 17 December 2013. http://www.cnbc.com/2013/12/17/whole-goods-seeks-to-expand-to-1200-store-in-us-alone.html.

39 Elon Musk, 'The Tesla approach to distributing and servicing cars,' *Tesla Motors*, 22 October 2012. http://www.teslamotors.com/blog/tesla-approach-distributing-and-servicing-cars.

40 'Find us,' *Tesla Motors*. http://www.teslamotors.com/findus/list/stores/United+States.

41 Callum Borchers, 'Automaker Tesla looks to bypass car dealers,' *Boston Globe*, 20 November, 2013. http://www.bostonglobe.com/business/2013/11/20/tesla-battles-auto-dealers-direct-sales-consumers/3f1xBFN21xH8QqQc3jijTP/story.html.

42 Musk, 'The Tesla approach to distributing and servicing cars.'

43 John Voelcker, 'Tesla loses legal battles to Texas, North Caroline dealers,' *Green Car Reports*, 6 June, 2013. http://www.greencarreports.com/news/1084622_tesla-loses-legal-battles-to-texas-north-carolina-dealers.

44 Ronald J. Hansen, 'Tesla pushes bill to bypass Ariz. car dealers,' *The Republic*, 5 February, 2015. http://www.azcentral.com/story/news/arizona/politics/2015/02/04/tesla-pushes-bill-arizona-car-dealers/22902857/.

45 Dana Hull, 'Tesla wants to power Walmart,' *Bloomberg*, 22 April, 2015. http://www.bloomberg.com/news/articles/2015-04-22/tesla-powered-wal-mart-stores-attest-to-musk-s-energy-ambitions.

46 'SGIP background,' *Center for Sustainable Energy*. https://energycenter.org/programs/self-generation-incentive-program/background.

47 Hull, 'Tesla wants to power Walmart.'

48 Maurizio Naldi and Marta Flamini, 'The CR4 index and the interval estimation of the Herfindahl–Hirschman Index: an empirical comparison,' 17 June, 2014, HAL ID: hal-01008144. https://halshs.archives-ouvertes.fr/hal-01008144/document.

49 Ibrahim Yucel, *IBISWorld Industry Report 81232: Dry Cleaners in the US*, Santa Monica, CA: IBISWorld, April, 2015.

50 'Tide Dry Cleaners opens first location in Draper, UT,' *PR Newswire*, 28 August, 2015.

51 Ibid.

52 Jim Gallagher, 'Can Tide Dry Cleaners clean up St. Louis?,' *St. Louis Post-Dispatch*, 10 February, 2013.

53 Andrew Martin, 'A trusted name in laundry seeks to crack dry-cleaning code,' *International Herald Tribune*, 10 December, 2010.

54 Andrew Martin, 'Smelling an opportunity,' *New York Times*, 8 December, 2010. http://www.nytimes.com/2010/12/09/business/09tide.html?_r=0.

55 Serena Ng and Paul Ziobro, 'P&G unveils plan for a budget tide,' *Wall Street Journal*, 4 September 2013. http://www.wsj.com/articles/SB10001424127887323623304579054894090748198.

56 'Tide Dry Cleaners opens first location in Draper, UT,' *PR Newswire*.

57 Jenn Abelson, 'High-concept cleaner in tatters,' *The Boston Globe*, 15 May, 2008.

58 Ibid.

59 Pierre Omidyar, 'Founders letter,' 26 February, 1996. http://pages.ebay.com/services/forum/feedback-foundersnote.html.

60 Pierre Omidyar, 'How Pierre Omidyar turned an idealistic notion into billions of dollars,' *Inc. Magazine*, 9 December, 2013. http://www.inc.com/magazine/201312/pierre-omidyar/ebay-inspiration-more-effective-than-delegation.html.

61 Patricia O'Connell, 'Online extra: Pierre Omidyar on "connecting people",' *Bloomberg*, 20 June, 2005. http://www.bloomberg.com/bw/stories/2005-06-19/online-extra-pierre-omidyar-on-connecting-people.

62 'Interview: Pierre Omidyar,' 27 October, 2000. http://www.achievement.org/autodoc/printmember/omioint-1.

63 Omidyar, 'Founders letter.'

64 Omidyar, 'How Pierre Omidyar turned an idealistic notion into billions of dollars.'

65 Mark Leibovich, 'Ebay attracts devoted following,' *Washington Post*, 31 January, 1999. http://www.washingtonpost.com/wp-srv/washtech/daily/jan99/ebay31.htm.

66 'Ebay soars to new heights,' 29 January, 1999. http://pages.ebay.com/aboutebay/thecompany/1999/january.html.

67 'Interview: Pierre Omidyar.'

68 John Bladon and Paul R. Daugherty, 'Newgame.com: changing rules in the utilities industry,' *Electric Light & Power*, April, 2000, p. 32.

69 Omidyar, 'How Pierre Omidyar turned an idealistic notion into billions of dollars.'

70 David Moschella, 'Online auctions: the exception – not the rule,' *Computerworld*, 19 July, 1999, p. 33.

71 Deidre McMurdy, 'Garage sales of the 'Net spell end of bargains,' CTV Television, 28 May, 1999.

72 Daniel Gross, 'Economy: Making a living on eBay,' *Newsweek*, 22 May, 2008. http://www.news-week.com/economy-making-living-ebay-89921.

73 Mark Albright, 'What's happened to all the flea markets?,' *St. Petersburg Times*, 24 February, 2008.

74 'It's nifty to be thrifty,' *Daily News of Los Angeles*, 25 July, 2010.

75 Transcript of eBay presentation at the Piper Jaffray Consumer Conference, 5 June, 2012.

76 David Carr, 'An interview with Pierre Omidyar,' *New York Times*, 20 October, 2013.

77 Shulevitz, 'Don't you dare say "disruptive".'

5   Developing the corporate business plan

A key ingredient for successful corporate venturing is developing a business plan for each new venture and process. This is what many entrepreneurial companies such as Apple Inc. do over and over again.

Scenario: Apple Inc.

In the late 2000s, Apple was considered one of the most innovative companies in the world. Its innovative success came following a near collapse after Apple produced no profits in the 1990s. How did such an innovative company create an astounding turnaround? The Apple Computer Company was founded in April 1976 by Steve Wozniak, Steve Jobs and Ron Wayne with $1,300 as a start-up in the garage of the Jobs family in Palo Alto, California. The initial 50 orders for the Apple I occurred the next month. By August, investors were lined up; Mike Markkula, who was an angel investor and later the second CEO of Apple, invested $92,000 in the company. The company progressively grew in the number of employees, the quantity of computers sold and the cost at which it was selling them. In May 1980, the Apple II was released and sold for up to $7,800. On 12 December of that year, Apple Computer went public; the company's share price rose by 32 percent that day making the 40 current employees millionaires.

Apple reached $1 billion in sales in 1982 and became the highest earning firm in personal computers. In May 1983, Apple's success continued as it became a member of the Fortune 500 and in December released the Apple III+, which sold for $2,995. In 1985, the same year Steve Jobs was removed from his position, the company sold 500,000 Macintoshes.

By the early 1990s, Apple's products faced significant competition from Microsoft, IBM, Motorola and NeXT (Steve Jobs's new company). In

1993, Apple began losing money and did not have profitability again until 1998.

In 1996, the year of Apple's twentieth anniversary, the company bought Steve Jobs's NeXT company for $340 million, and by early 1997, Jobs was back at Apple. Later that year, the Mac Operating System 8 was released and 1.25 million copies were sold in less than two weeks. This made oS8 the best-selling software of the time.

Apple was once again profitable in 1998 with $47 million in profits in the first quarter alone. The iMac and PowerBook G3 models were introduced and seen by many as the most innovative machines in the world. In addition, Jobs refocused Apple's business plan by targeting personal and business consumers who desired portable or desktop computers. Second quarter profits in 1998 were $101 million.

Also in 1998, Apple started creating products not totally associated with computers: iMovie and Final Cut Pro were released serving the digital video editing market. A few months later, music productivity applications, namely Emagic and GarageBand, were released.

The company really took off in 2001 when the Apple Retail Store opened in Virginia and later that year when Apple introduced the iPod. In 2003, the iTunes store was created allowing users to download songs to their iPods for approximately $0.99 per song. By mid 2008, customers had downloaded over five billion songs.

In 2007, Apple officially changed its name from Apple Computers to Apple Inc. and began producing the iPhone as well as Apple TV. Once App Stores were opened in July 2008, the company was selling roughly $1 million a day and a few months later had become ranked as the third largest supplier of mobile handsets.

There is not much doubt that Steve Jobs's leadership and highly skilled engineers played a significant role in Apple's comeback, but it took more than programming talent and a good CEO to create such spectacular success. It was the company's focus on innovation and a unique company culture that encouraged a leap in product innovation (iPhone, Apple TV, iPods), putting Apple ahead of the curve and, in some instances, ahead of its time.

Several key aspects made Apple particularly successful in its move to greatness. Apple uses what it calls 'Network Innovation.' This process has the ability to tie together ideas from the outside with Apple's own twists and charm. The iPod, for example, was envisioned by a consultant. The product simply combined already existing external, off-the-shelf technologies and added a unique, elegant and stylish design. By recognizing that not all great ideas are born within the company, Apple was able to avoid the 'not invented here' syndrome where in-house ideas and creations are valued more than those from outside the company.

Internal innovation also calls for a strategy that includes using a business plan approach. According to Steve Jobs, it requires more than just discipline, processes and procedures to invent and create great products. It requires a laid back, horizontal culture where employees know each other and meet in the hallway or feel comfortable calling each other at 10:30 p.m. to discuss a new idea or an ongoing project. The company has created a culture where employees are not afraid to speak up and call an ad hoc meeting among six colleagues to receive feedback on a brand new idea. According to Jobs, it takes 1,000 good ideas to come up with one great one.

While many companies focus on the demands of technology, Apple structured itself internally to have the ability to understand and focus on the needs of users. Rather than making yet another digital music player that required the skills of an engineer in order to use it, Apple focused on the desires and needs of the non-engineer users. When technology firms, including Apple's competitors, strove to develop the more complex, Apple distinguished itself, its innovation strategies and its products by appealing to a mass audience through straightforward, easy-to-use products.

Contrary to the usual market beliefs, Apple ensured its incredible comeback by NOT listening to the market. Ironically, had Apple engaged in 'user-centric innovation' (adapting product designs to customer feedback), it may have never produced the iPod. The iPod was so innovative with such a unique development that upon its launch in 2001, it was considered ludicrous.

Just as a culture of innovation is important to corporate venturing, so is the ability to fail wisely. Rather than stigmatizing failure, Apple has created an environment where failure is both tolerated and seen as a company-wide learning and enrichment experience.

Introduction

Every successful and innovative company follows its own path to success. The strategies used by Apple may not work for every organization attempting to be innovative; Apple followed its own rules and created its own culture. Having a culture that emphasizes and supports innovation with creative out-of-the-box thinking is essential for establishing a successful corporate venturing program. An equally important aspect is the evaluation of the idea created through the creation of a business plan, the focus of this chapter.

The chapter starts by giving an overview of the importance of a business plan followed by a discussion of its scope and value. Following the informational needs for the plan is a thorough description of each of its major aspects. The chapter concludes by presenting the uses and implementation of the business plan and why they often fail.

Importance of a business plan

In any organization, there are a variety of plans – financial plans, marketing plans, production/operation plans, sales plans and staffing plans. A plan can be strategic or operational and focus on the short or long term. Regardless of its scope, each plan provides guidance and structure for success.

A corporate venture business plan is a document describing all relevant external and internal elements involved in launching a corporate venture or process. It is often an integration of various functional plans that address both short- and long-term decisions for at least the first five years of operation.

Many entrepreneurial Third Party Administration (TPA) firm owners might argue that they've operated for years successfully without a business plan. In a nutshell – that was then, and this is now! We live and work in a rapidly changing world. Our industry is directly impacted by the economy, tax legislation, regulation and technological changes. It is extremely important to have a plan and a system to measure success. A business plan forces you to look inward with a critical eye and identify your strengths and weaknesses. It also requires you to look outward and perform an environmental scan, analyzing the industry, the competition and identifying potential opportunities and threats.[1]

As a game plan or road map, the business plan is as important as planning a trip from Phoenix, Arizona to Vienna, Austria when there are a number of possible routes and airlines available, each having its own timeframe and costs. The traveler, like the corporate entrepreneur, needs to gather external information and make the most appropriate decision determined in part by the availability of time and money. Like the traveler, the corporate entrepreneur needs to prepare the business plan for the corporate venturing activity using any resources available in the organization.

Scope and value of the business plan

The individuals creating the corporate business plan need to be prepared to address issues, needs and concerns of each constituency in the organization. While these individuals will definitely include management of the organization and/or the internal venture fund's evaluation team, they could also include consultants, customers, employees, suppliers or rarely even outside funders.

The corporate entrepreneur needs to put him or herself in the position of the potential buyer. Apple's tremendous turnaround in 1998 (with its focus on desktop and portable computers) and continued success in 2009 (with the simple-to-use iPod) was a direct result of considering the product from the end users' point of view.

The business plan is valuable to the corporate entrepreneur as it: (1) establishes the objectives and goals of the proposed corporate venture; (2) provides guidance about the needs and planning necessary for implementing the corporate venture; (3) helps determine the viability of the corporate venture in the organization; and (4) provides the information necessary to obtain management approval and funding.

The original plan frequently needs to be revised by focusing on such questions as: Does the idea really have value? Who is the customer and will they purchase it? Who are the competitors and is there any protection against competitive threats? Can I really manage the corporate entrepreneurial venture? Do I really want to do this?

The corporate business plan

Most corporate business plans are tailored to the needs of the organization particularly reflecting its goals, products/services offered and industry. While the plans are indeed organizational specific, most contain many of the aspects indicated in Table 5.1. In general, corporate business plans start with an executive summary followed by specific details of the plan such as the product/service analysis, corporate fit, market analysis, marketing plan, profitability and plan for future actions, each of which are discussed in turn.

Executive summary

The executive summary is written following the completion of the plan. It is usually no more than two to three pages in length although some companies want only one page. As the name implies, it summarizes the entire plan by highlighting in a concise, convincing manner the major parts of the corporate business plan. Of particular importance to the corporate readers are a brief description of the unique value proposition of the product/service, the degree of corporate fit and the market size, trends and growth rate.

Product/service analysis

This section focuses on the various aspects of the product/service idea. This requires a detailed description of the product/service idea and how it fulfills the market need. Where appropriate, a prototype or detailed design helps ensure complete understanding of the concept. Regardless of what is included, it is necessary to clearly and thoroughly delineate the specific aspects of the idea. Any product limitations should also be discussed as well as the type and extent of product liability. The analysis should also cite any specific government approvals needed and the obtainment process.

The product/service analysis can be looked at under the following subheadings:

1. Product differentiation
2. Product description
3. Product demonstration.

Table 5.1 Corporate business plan

Executive Summary

Product/Service Analysis
- Purpose of the product/service
- Stage of development
- Product limitation
- Proprietary rights
- Government approvals
- Product liability
- Related services and spin-offs
- Production

Corporate Fit
- Product fit into corporate goals
- Customer base
- Utilization of assets
- Staff needs
- Distribution fit

Market Analysis
- Current market size
- Growth potential of the market
- Industry trends
- Competition profile
- Customer profile
- Customer benefits
- Market segment(s)
- Target market(s)

Marketing Plan
- Product
- Price
- Supply chain (distribution channels)
- Promotion

Profitability
- Pro forma income statements
- Capital expenditures

Plan for Further Action
- Problems
- Benefits
- Corporate management and staff needed

Product differentiation

One aspect to consider is product differentiation, focusing on the aspects of a product that make it different and unique. Each product can be placed somewhere on a commodity/specialty continuum with commodity products having few, if any, perceived differences (mainly competing on claims and price) and specialty products having many differences to the point of being unique and possibly able to capture a price premium. For a commodity product, profitability will depend on a company's ability to offer a price favorable to that of its competitor's. In order to achieve this, the company needs to be highly skilled in machine design and able to reduce labor costs. The opposite talents are needed for a specialty product whose profitability depends on the knowledge and application of marketing, an approach centered on the determination and execution of a unique selling proposition.

To build an image of uniqueness, there needs to be an individualized name supported by advertisements and an innovative sales message. Two companies that have done this successfully are General Foods with minute rice and Quaker Oats with oatmeal. General Foods made its long-grain rice a specialty product when there were more than 20 products competing at about the same price point. Likewise, in 2009, Quaker Oats integrated the 'super grain' aspect and the heart healthy benefit of eating this product.

One way of converting a commodity product into a more specialty item is to process a product in a unique way that adds increased value for the customer. A second way of converting a commodity product to a more specialty item is to add something to the actual product that is desired by the consumer and differentiates the product from others in that commodity category. Miller, in heavy competition with many other companies making similar beers, eliminated calories in its Lite Beer.

Miller's strategy makes an interesting comparison to the successful product differentiation of one of its competitors, Dos Equis. The 'Most Interesting Man in the World' campaign increased market share especially in markets outside the United States, its home country. This campaign further strengthened the competitive advantage of Dos Equis by using social media over the traditional television commercials.

A third method of changing a commodity product into a specialty one is by 'being the firstest with the mostest.' This establishes the first mover advantage. In this strategy, the company determines something unique about its commodity product that is beneficial to the consumer and has not been previously available. Even though competitive products can have the same qualities in their product, by being first and consistent in advertising, a company can establish that its product really possesses these qualities.

Wonder Bread did this very well when the company started its advertisement – 'Wonder Bread Builds Strong Bodies in 12 Different Ways' – indicating the combination of 12 minerals and vitamins, any competitor could have claimed the same attributes. By being first, Wonder Bread uniquely positioned itself as the trendsetter and original builder of strong bodies in the bread category.

A fourth way of changing a commodity product into a specialty one is through packaging, or a combination of package and brand name. Even though the components of salt are the same throughout the industry, Morton's patented spout (the patent rights have now run out), combined with informing the consumer about the uniqueness of 'When it Rains, it Pours,' moved the company's salt from a commodity category to more of a specialty product.

An example of combining package and brand name is Janitor in a Drum. The drum, made to look like an industrial drum, combined with the name implies that this floor detergent is stronger than others. It was marketed as an intensive cleaner that takes some of the work away from the consumer as if an actual janitor had cleaned the area.

A final method of converting a commodity product into a specialty item is by structuring the product differently. This occurred for a quinine-flavored soda pop that was restructured into Schweppes Tonic Water, a product used to mix alcoholic beverages. A similar tactic was used by Warner–Lambert upon acquiring Hall's Candy Company. Hall's was making 40 commodity candy items, none doing well, and was losing money. One of these commodity candy items was restructured as a cough drop, with the slogan, 'It helps you breathe easier.' The item was successfully introduced as Hall's Mentho-Lyptus in the United States.

Product description

There are several other things to consider in describing the product/ service idea brand name, trademark, logo and patents. A manufacturer's brand is when the registered name is owned by the company making the product. This name may be an umbrella name, a category name or a specific product name. A family brand name – also referred to as a corporate name, umbrella or family brand – is a brand name placed on all products sold by a firm. Borden is a firm that utilizes a family brand name to cover its many diversified commodity products from pastas to soups to adhesives.

A category brand name is a brand name used on a common category of products. Firms that use a category name usually have several category brand names. An example is Sears with 'Kenmore' products for household appliances. A specific product name is a brand name used on one and only one product. When specific product names are assigned to a second product, it is frequently the start of a category name.

A trademark gives the firm the exclusive right of ownership on all goods associated with the trademark. The name Kodak, awarded to Eastman Kodak, belongs to the company and cannot be used by anyone else on similar products. Kleenex is another trademark example that has worked its way into everyday language to describe a tissue rather than the brand.

A logo is a letter, symbol or sign used to represent the entire word or words of the trademark. These can also be registered with the federal government and used on an exclusive basis. While the picture of Aunt Jemima on a syrup bottle is a logo, the words Aunt Jemima are a trademark. Visual symbols are a valuable way to translate the company's message and brand across language barriers.

While patents are not granted on brand names, they are granted on: (1) unique ideas that contribute something new to the state of the art or (2) new materials or ingredients that have not been used before but that can be used as a substitute for the original material or ingredient established in the art. Patents can also be held on the machinery used in the actual production of the product itself. For example, the spout on Morton Salt was patented.

In selecting a meaningful brand name, the company needs to avoid geographic words. Many companies have regretted taking the name of a city, a country, a river or a valley as they found out later that others also have a right to this name. One classic example of this is the original 'Smithfield Hams,' a name based on the town of its location, Smithfield, Virginia. At one time, there were three 'Smithfield Hams' made by different companies because the original 'Smithfield Hams' could not be solely used as Smithfield was a geographic location.

Another category of brand names that the organization needs to avoid is generic terms. A generic category is one that identifies homogeneous products concerning composition and/or use. For example, sodium acetylsalicylic acid is the generic term for aspirin tablets. When a name becomes generic, anyone can use that name. It is also risky to use a word whose pronunciation is similar to that of a word used to describe products in a particular category. Miller beer made this mistake with the name 'Lite,' which is pronounced like 'light,' a word commonly used to describe beers. Any beer manufacturer has the right to use the same term, which was the strategy used by Anheuser-Busch and Amstel.

Even though Coca-Cola fought for years to maintain its name, the courts forced the company to relinquish half of its name, 'cola,' feeling it was a generic beverage name allowing others to have similar rights. This made a wide variety of colas available such as Pepsi Cola.

Often a new product can be effectively linked to a proven brand name, thereby decreasing the odds of failure. By using the recognizable asset of a proven name, many companies have successfully entered new markets and introduced new products. Examples of this include Bic Roller pen, Levi's skirts and shoes, Del Monte Mexican Food, Easy-Off window cleaner and Vaseline Intensive Care skin lotion, bath oil and baby powder. However, this does not necessarily guarantee success. Such failures as Arm and Hammer Antiperspirant, Certs Gum and Listerine household cleaner illustrate that a strong name in one category does not necessarily guarantee success in another.

While there are many criteria that can be used in selecting and establishing a brand name, the most important ones are pronunciation, connotation and memorability.

A brand name should be easily pronounced and in only one way in a given market. This aspect can be tested by printing the proposed name in 1- to 2-inch type on white cardboard and presenting the name for pronunciation to a sample in the market. It is important to keep this pronunciation and name as consistent as possible when entering new markets with different cultures and languages. In 2009, Pepsi Cola changed its long-time name Pepsi to Pecsi to better accommodate the pronunciation of its brand in Argentina.

A name that is easily remembered is most desirable because it needs to stick in the minds of consumers. This can be determined by selecting the 30 best names and telling a sample of consumers that the 30 names are to be used on a 'name category of a product' (such as a grocery item, pharmaceutical product or hardware product). Each name is then presented on a card and pronounced for the consumer sample. Each person is asked to write down the most remembered names with the name recalled most frequently in each product category being the most memorable.

Product demonstration

A final area to consider is the packaging. The product's final packaging mix is important in a variety of ways. A good packaging mix is one that creates consistency for the product's brand message, protects the product, adapts to production line speeds, promotes or sells the product, increases the product density, facilitates the use of the product, provides reusable value to the consumer, satisfies legal requirements, is eco-friendly and keeps the packaging costs as low as possible.

The consumer package is the package that is purchased and taken home by the consumer. At times, the consumer package is made so that it can be put on display for the consumer at the retail level and used at home for other purposes.

The shipping case is the container in which the product is shipped and stored in the warehouse. It is packed either with display boxes, as in the case of Alka-Seltzer retail boxes, with consumer packages such as Pillsbury cake mix boxes or with bulk products such as kegs of nails.

The first requisite of a good packaging design is that it protects the product, according to the needs of each product. If the product is perishable, the manufacturer needs to have temperature and humidity charts for each marketed area of the product.

Packaging can also be used simultaneously to achieve product uniqueness as well as product protection. The Morton Salt pour spout, which was a convenience to the consumer, also protected the salt from moisture by sealing the package after usage. Frequently, the packaging innovations are developed by the packing material manufacturers. Procter & Gamble, working with Container Corporation of America, introduced the protective composite can used today for snack items such as Pringles and Cheetos.

A packaging innovation sold to the wine industry is the Mega-Cask, a bag-in-a-box container. The special container saves money for restaurants, hotels and clubs by preserving the quality of wine while allowing faster, more efficient serving.

The final task of the package is to sell the product to the consumer. Four general merchandising principles are important: apparent size; attention-drawing power; impression of quality; and brand name readability.

When a product is displayed among a myriad of competing products, a package should have the ability to capture and hold the attention of the targeted consumer. What gives a package this power? The package design – the combination of elements – that together produces attractiveness, purity, appetite appeal and high quality and gives the package attention-drawing power is the one sought often. Breakfast cereals for children have two target markets, children and parents. The children are the end consumers but the parent(s) make the final purchasing decision. Companies such as Kellogg's take this into consideration by including on its packaging the colorful, fun images sought out by children and the nutritional value desired by parents.

Whenever appropriate (such as in the case of food products), a picture of the product should be displayed on the front panel in an appetizing manner. Nothing attracts and holds interest more than pictures of a food product.

A package needs to convey the feeling of quality. One way to test this is to evaluate the finished package against several good and bad product qualities. The company should always make sure that the package printing does not appear washed-out or faded as this gives an impression of an older product with poor quality. Printing needs to be bright but not gaudy.

The brand name on a package should be easily readable. Readability is especially important in the case of packages that are distributed through large self-service outlets since these packages must compete with numerous items in the same product class in relatively restricted shelf areas. To achieve readability, it is important to make the letters as large as possible using the same print used in large daily paper headlines. If the new idea is a manufacturing operation, there is a need for an initial production plan. This plan should describe the complete manufacturing process.

Corporate fit

An important aspect of the product/service idea is that it supports the mission statement, direction and focus of the company. This part of the corporate business plan clearly differentiates it from an entrepreneurial start-up business plan. The better the idea fulfills the corporate goals and utilizes the assets of the company, the more likely it will receive favorable attention. Other fits that make the idea more attractive include selling to the same customer base, using the same distribution system and using the existing employee expertise in making, delivering and marketing the idea.

Market analysis

This section of the corporate business plan can be the most difficult to prepare particularly for individuals from the technical side of the organization. Some companies help reduce this problem by providing a workshop on market analysis, information sources and the marketing plan. This workshop provides a better understanding for writing an effective corporate business plan and makes people aware of the importance of market analysis.

The market analysis should focus on the market need for the idea. The identified market should address size, trends (the last three years), growth rate and characteristics. In addition, this section needs to focus on identifying all products/services and the companies that presently serve this need.

The various sources of information such as general information, industry and market information, competitive company and product information, search engines, and trade associations and publications are found in Chapter 3 of this volume.

Market segmentation

This market information provides the basis for doing significant market segmentation for the new product/service idea. Table 5.2 lists the six overall segmentation criteria that can be used along with their specific applications in each of the three major markets: business-to-consumer

Table 5.2   Market segmentation by type of market

Segmentation Criteria	Basis for Type of Market		
	Business-to-Consumer	Business-to-Business	Business-to-Government
Demographic	education level, income, nationality, occupation, age, race, gender	number of employees, size of sales, size of profit, type of product lines	type of agency, size of budget, amount of autonomy
Geographic	region of country, city, country	country, region of country	federal, state, local
Psychological	personality traits, motives, lifestyle	degree of industrial leadership	degree of forward thinking
Benefits	durability, dependability, economy, esteem enhancement, status from ownership, handiness	dependability, reliability of seller and support service, efficiency in operation or use, enhancement of firm's earning, durability	dependability, reliability of seller and support services
Volume of use	heavy, medium, light	heavy, medium, light	heavy, medium, light
Controllable marketing elements	sales promotion, price, advertising, guarantee, warranty, product attributes, reputation of seller	price, service, warranty, reputation of seller	price, reputation of seller

(B2C), business-to-business (B2B) or business-to-government (B2G). The two most frequently used segmentation techniques are demographic and geographic, which also have the most published secondary data available, the sources of which were discussed previously. The most widely used consumer demographic variables are income, gender and age while the most widely used industrial variables are type of product lines and sales. These can be used on any defined geographic region.

Other less used techniques include psychological benefits, volume of use and controllable marketing elements. Of these, the segmentation variable producing the most effective results is benefit segmentation. While in Table 5.2 generic benefits are listed such as durability, dependability, reliability, economy, status from ownership and efficiency in operation for use in the B2C and B2B, the organization should determine the exact benefits the customer wants through market research. When these benefits match the unique selling propositions of the product/service being considered, there is an even better chance of a successful launch.

Marketing plan

The marketing plan needs to be based on the market analysis and market segmentation for the idea. This fourth area of the corporate business plan needs to be developed in terms of four major areas: product/service mix; price mix; distribution mix; and promotion mix as indicated in Figure 5.1. Each element has its own mix to fill the market need and achieve customer satisfaction. These elements need to be aimed at the satisfaction of the target group of customers, which requires that the customer be the hub and focal point of all the firm's activities. Customer wants and needs should be analyzed enabling the company's offering to match these – the essence of the marketing concept.

The product/service area includes all the aspects that make up the physical product or service. Decisions need to be made on quality, assortment, breadth and depth of line, warranty, guarantee, service and packaging. All these characteristics make the final product or service more (or less) appealing to the target market.[2]

Closely related to the product and its mix is the price. While probably the least understood of the elements, the price of the product greatly influences the image of the product as well as the product's purchase potential. The established price needs to take into consideration the three C's: cost, competition and consumer.

An illustration of the effect of price by channel of distribution members is indicated in Figure 5.2. As shown, every time a channel member is added, the percentage margin increases the final selling price for the consumer. While the cheapest price is obtained by not using any channel members, as in the case of direct, mail order or web-based

Figure 5.1 Marketing plan

sales, often channel members are needed for successful sales. Channel members often have better access to the targeted market segment and can facilitate relations with the end customer.

The third basic element of the marketing mix – distribution – covers two different areas. The first area – channels of distribution – deals with the institutions such as wholesalers and retailers that deliver the product from the firm into the hands of the consumer. Physical distribution, the second area, deals with the aspects of physically moving the product from the firm to the consumer. This includes such things as warehouse, inventory and transportation. This part of the marketing plan is often not required in a corporate business plan particularly if the company's present channel and system will be used.

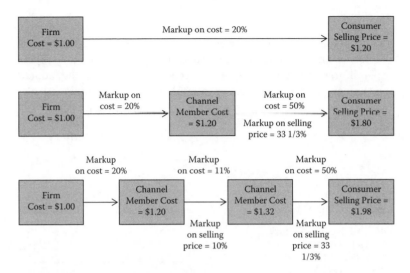

Figure 5.2   Channel members and the price

The final element – promotion – involves policies and procedures related to five areas:

1. Personal selling: emphasis on personal selling and the methods employed in the manufacturer's organization and in the trade often used in businesses such as car dealerships, pharmaceuticals and residential construction.
2. Advertising: policies and procedures relating to budget, message and media such as television, radio, print ads and so on.
3. Promotions: policies and procedures relating to budget, types of consumer deals, trade promotions and in store displays.
4. Publicity: policies and procedures relating to a comprehensive program for effective media coverage and a strong company image.
5. Social media: media such as Facebook, Twitter, banner ads, viral commercials and so on that can be used to successfully relate the value and benefits of the new product or service to the targeted consumers.

Again, for similar reasons as distribution, this is often not required at least in the initial corporate business plan.

Profitability

The profitability section of the corporate business plan focuses on the pro forma income statement indicated in Figure 5.3 and any capital expenditures on equipment that are needed in developing and launching the new product/service. An example of these and other calculations of a pro forma income statement are shown in Figure 5.4.

Three-year Summary

	Year 1	Year 2	Year 3
TOTAL REVENUE[a]			
Less: COST OF GOODS SOLD[b]			
GROSS PROFIT (Margin)			
OPERATING EXPENSES:			
Management Salaries			
Fringe Benefits			
Other Salaries			
Other Fringe Benefits			
Consultant			
Advertising & Promotion			
Delivery			
Bad Debts			
General Administration Expense			
Legal Expenses			
Rent			
Utilities			
Insurance			
Taxes and Licensing			
Interest			
Outsource Accounting & Payroll			
Depreciation			
Miscellaneous			
_____			
_____			
TOTAL OPERATING EXPENSES			
PROFIT (LOSS) PRE-TAX			
TAXES			
NET PROFIT (LOSS)			

Notes:
a. The calculation of the Total Revenue should be shown with references to the marketing plan.
b. The cost of Goods Sold should be broken down into its components on a separate table, and its final calculation shown.

Figure 5.3 Pro forma income statement

ASSUMING:
1. 1400 units sold
2. Price = $40
3. Cost = $10

TOTAL REVENUE:
Units × Price 1400 × 40 $56,000.00

Less: Cost of Goods Sold
Units × Cost 1400 × 10   14,000.00

GROSS PROFIT (Margin)   **$42,000.00**

OPERATING EXPENSES:
Salary	$60,000.00
Fringe Benefit 25%	15,000.00
Rent & Shared Office Answering Service	3,600.00
($300/month)	
Electricity ($70/month)	840.00
Gas ($20/month)	240.00
Legal (startup expenses)	4,000.00
Manufacturer's Representative	2,800.00
(5% of sales price to retail $40)	
(1400 × 40 × 5%)	
Advertising (from advertising budget)	40,000.00
Telephone (unlimited cell phone)	1,200.00
($100/month)	
Consultant ($3000/month)	36,000.00
Outsourcing Accounting & Payroll	900.00
($75/month)	

TOTAL OPERATING EXPENSES   **$164,580.00**

NET PROFIT (Loss)   **($122,584.00)**

TAXES   **$0.00**

NET PROFIT (Loss)   **($122,580.00)**

Figure 5.4   Example of pro forma income statement

Plan for further action

The corporate business plan should end with a brief section called the Plan for Further Action. This section addresses any potential problems in developing and marketing the idea as well as the expected benefits for the organization. The manager should also pay special attention to acquiring external information and knowledge as market uncertainty was pointed out as the biggest obstacle to business planning.[3] This section concludes with a general discussion about the size and type of corporate management and staff needed to develop and successfully launch the idea. This final section usually is not very specific.

Summary

This chapter has focused on the corporate business plan. While the format and requirements of the business plan are almost always company specific, some areas usually occurring are discussed. The major aspects of a corporate business plan – executive summary, product/service analysis, corporate fit, market analysis, market segmentation, marketing plan, profitability and plan for further action – are covered along with its importance and use.

NOTES

1 Sarah Simoneaux and Chris Stroud, 'A business plan: the GPS for your company,' *Journal of Pension Benefits: Issues in Administration,* **18** (2), Winter, 2011, 92–5.

2 For further reading, see 'How to develop a new product plan,' in Roman Hiebling, Scott Cooper and Steve Wehrenberg, *The Successful Marketing Plan: How to Create Dynamic, Results-oriented Marketing* (4th edn), 2012, Chapter 12, pp. 327–8.

3 Inkon Koh and Dae Ho Kim, 'A study on the relationship between business plan components and corporate performance,' *International Journal of Entrepreneurship and Innovation Management,* **8** (4), 2008, 359–80.

Online sources

http://www.apple.com/pr/.

http://www.businessweek.com/innovate/content/jun2010/id20100610_525759.htm.

Scenario: Textron Ltd

Textron started as a small textile company in 1923, when 27-year-old Royal Little founded the Special Yarns Corporation in Boston, Massachusetts. Revenues in the first year were $75,000. Today the company has grown into a highly successful multi-industry enterprise recognized for its network of powerful brands, world-class processes and talented people.

Textiles boomed during World War II, ushering in a period of growth and activity for the company. A major line of business during the war was parachutes. In 1943, with government contracts dwindling, Little faced the challenge of declining revenue and underutilized production capacity. He developed a vertically integrated company that controlled every operational aspect from raw goods processing to distribution. He moved quickly from producing parachutes to making lingerie, blouses, bed linen and other consumer goods. Marking a major milestone for the company, Textron was listed on the New York Stock Exchange on 22 December 1947. By 1949, Textron's sales had reached $67.8 million.

In 1952, facing yet another decline in the demand for textiles Little approached the Textron Board of Directors for approval to diversify by acquiring businesses in unrelated industries. He planned to maintain textile operations as an earnings base while acquiring non-textile businesses. In 1953, Textron purchased its first non-textile business, Burkart Manufacturing Co. in Missouri. This company supplied cushioning materials to the automotive market. Little's success in building a diversified company prompted other businesses to follow his model. Textron avoided many of the costly mistakes of other conglomerates by entering new lines of business with small, incremental investments, where other conglomerates tended to make massive acquisitions.

The pace of acquisitions was great and among the more important businesses added in the early 1950s were Homelite, which was retained until 1994, Camcar, which was retained until 2006, and CWC, which remains part of Textron today. In 1960, Textron purchased Bell Aerospace – which included Bell Helicopter – to balance Textron's earnings base by increasing its government business. At the same time, Little added another company, which, like Bell, remains a part of Textron: golf car manufacturer E-Z-GO. Textron's founder, Royal Little, retired as chairman at the end of 1960. Sales had grown to $383 million. Little's successor, banker Rupert Thompson, led Textron into the new decade alongside company President G. William Miller. In 1963, Textron sold its last textile operation.

Consumer product businesses defined Textron in the 1960s and 1970s. Notable acquisitions during this period included Speidel, maker of watchbands, Sheaffer Pen, staple and nail gun maker, Bostich and Rhode Island silver company, Gorham. Throughout this period, Textron was recognized as the pioneer of the conglomerate and one of the most highly diversified corporations in the Unites States. In 1967, the *Wall Street Journal* called Textron 'the conglomerate king.' During this time, Textron common stock also split twice: once in January 1966 and again in September 1967.

William Miller succeeded Thompson as CEO at the end of 1968. Acquisitions under Miller included snowmobile maker, Polaris, Australian card maker, Valentine Holdings and the venture capital firm, American Research & Development. Miller's tenure at Textron ended in 1977, when President Jimmy Carter nominated him to be Chairman of the Federal Reserve. He later served as Secretary of the Treasury for President Carter. Joseph Collinson succeeded Miller as Textron's chairman and CEO. In 1979, Collinson retired, and he was succeeded by Robert P. Straetz as chairman and CEO. Beverly F. Dolan, founder and former president of E-Z-GO, was president. By the end of 1979, revenues reached $3.3 billion.

In October 1984, Textron emerged newly strengthened for growth in a reviving economy. Straetz and Dolan realized that the company could grow most effectively through strategic acquisitions. In February 1985, Textron acquired Avco Corporation, a conglomerate of almost equal size with pre-acquisition revenue of $2.9 billion. Overnight, with the addition of its Avco subsidiary, Textron nearly doubled in size. Dolan, who had become chairman in 1986 upon the retirement of

Straetz, initiated the second major acquisition of the decade that same year. Ex-Cell-O brought another $1.1 billion in annual sales from the aerospace, defense, automotive and industrial markets. This acquisition made Textron a major player in the automotive industry. Shortly thereafter, Textron common stock split for the third time in its history in June 1987.

In 1989, Dolan recruited James F. Hardymon as Textron's new president after a 28-year career at Emerson Electric. Hardymon quickly distinguished himself by his determination to design a more focused operating company that would produce consistent quarter-over-quarter earnings growth. He was named chairman and CEO in 1992. One of Hardymon's first actions as CEO was to acquire Cessna Aircraft Company. A leader in light and medium-sized commercial business jets, Cessna balanced Bell's significant defense-related business activity.

With a dual focus on operational improvement and portfolio management, Hardymon set out to maintain the record of consistent growth. From 1989 to the end of 1997, Textron decreased its holdings in military contracting, insurance and consumer products, divesting 'non-core' businesses with $2.8 billion in revenue while bolstering its 'core' by acquiring businesses totaling $3.9 billion in revenue. Over this time, the company migrated from deriving 56 percent of revenue from core businesses to obtaining 100 percent from the then-core of aircraft, automotive, industrial and finance. Textron also focused on increasing international revenue as a source of growth. In 1989, approximately 20 percent of Textron's revenue came from non-US operations. By the end of 1997, this figure had almost doubled.

Hardymon simultaneously focused on evolving Textron from a classic holding company to an operating company, distinguished as much for building and growing businesses as for buying and selling them. In 1994, following the acquisition of the plastics operations of Chrysler's Acustar Division, Textron's six automotive businesses were combined into one company, Textron Automotive Company. Similarly, in 1995, Textron Fastening Systems Inc. (TFS) was formed by merging five Textron fastening companies to form a global fastener group, making TFS the largest producer of engineered fastening products and solutions in the world.

Increasing teamwork among Textron's employees also became a priority. Cooperation among engineering, sales, marketing, product development, operations and other functions was fostered through councils, forums and meetings that brought together different businesses and segments. In May of 1997, Textron common stock split for the fourth time in its history.

In a well-defined succession planning process, Lewis B. Campbell was appointed CEO on 1 July 1998. Soon after his appointment, Campbell began engineering a new strategic framework for Textron aimed at strengthening financial performance during the good times and improving the company's ability to weather unforeseen economic headwinds and market downturns. Recognizing that an unprecedented transformation was essential, Campbell established Textron's Transformation Leadership Team (TLT) in 2000, composed of the top leaders from Textron and its business units. The team charter was: to advance Textron's new strategic framework to generate sustainable and compelling growth well into the future. Under Campbell's stewardship, the new vision for the corporation was to become the premier multi-industry company, recognized for its network of powerful brands, world-class enterprise processes and talented people.

Textron continued to make strategic divestitures and complementary acquisitions to strengthen its strategic portfolio, including the divestitures of its fastening systems business in August 2006, the sale of its fluid and power business in November 2008 and the sale of HR Textron in 2009. Meanwhile, Textron has continued to make acquisitions to complement its core businesses, including Overwatch Systems in 2006 and United Industrial Corporation (which owns AAI Corporation) in 2007. Also in 2007, Textron common stock split for the fifth time.

Textron's global brands – Bell, Cessna Aircraft, E-Z-GO, AAI Corporation, Lycoming Engines and Greenlee – are recognized for their innovative products. The innovations that they've brought to the markets have produced aircraft like the Bell-Boeing V-22 Osprey tiltorotor. Such innovation has also led to recent product launches, including Cessna's 162 SkyCatcher and Bell's Model 429. The E-Z-GO RXV has been a 'game-changer' with a golf car that delivers greater comfort and energy efficiency for customers. Jacobsen's Eclipse 322 hybrid riding greens is the first of its kind – free of hydraulics, easy to maintain and customized to meet the specific requirements of any golf course.

Campbell retired on 1 December 2009 and was succeeded by Scott C. Donnelly, who joined Textron in July 2008. Under Donnelly's leadership, Textron's steadfast execution of its financial and operational strategies continues to build value for its stakeholders. Combined with its portfolio of renowned brands and some of the most sophisticated and leading technology products in the world, there are tremendous opportunities ahead for Textron.

Introduction

The challenge facing many organizations today is how to develop a successful business approach that will contribute to successful corporate venturing. This requires selection and recruitment of individuals with entrepreneurial competencies, evaluation of their performance and providing equitable compensation and rewards that generate motivation.

The role of the corporate entrepreneur needs to be diverse. He or she must identify entrepreneurial opportunities and transform them into action. Corporate entrepreneurs need to constantly seek new venture opportunities. The corporate entrepreneur can monitor change and compete in a dynamic environment by using a corporate management checklist for evaluating the potential of creating a successful new corporate venture within the existing organization (Table 6.1). This chapter discusses the selection, evaluation and compensation of the corporate entrepreneur.

Selecting a corporate entrepreneur and a team

The single most important factor in the success of a corporate entrepreneurial activity is having a leader and a team with the ability and passion to transform ideas into reality. While selecting and retaining the right talent can be difficult, with the right incentives this can be accomplished. Jack Welch, former CEO of General Electric (GE), spent the last years of his tenure developing policies and practices that would enable GE to recruit, select and retain entrepreneurial individuals and develop the entrepreneurial potential needed among existing employees. Since usually no single individual possesses the wide variety of skills necessary to develop a corporate venture, the composition of the right team is needed. At Xerox New Enterprises, a division that commercializes novel technologies, the lead corporate entrepreneur of each new company is almost always recruited externally.

Table 6.1 Corporate checklist for evaluating the potential of creating a successful corporate entrepreneurial activity within the existing organization

Evaluation Criteria

Evaluate the venture potential in relation to the following criteria:	No	Uncertain	Yes
1. Has a business plan been developed?			
2. Is the business idea or concept feasible?			
3. Have financial statements and projections been prepared and discussed with the financial manager?			
4. Are there adequate financial resources available?			
5. Is the time required to reach positive cash flow realistic?			
6. Are the required human resources with the necessary skills and abilities available?			
7. Do the financial needs for the new venture match the capacity of the existing organization?			

Market Viability

Evaluate the market viability in relation to the following criteria:	Inadequate	Similar to competitors	Better than competitors	Excellent	Uncertain
1. Evaluate the potential of a viable and credible market opportunity.					
2. Assess the market approach including strategies for managing: customers • suppliers • competitors. • other external factors					
3. Evaluate the ability to create a successful business, while at the same time protecting the parent organization.					

Table 6.1 (continued)

Venture Management Criteria

Evaluate the venture management potential in relation to the following criteria:	No	Uncertain	Yes
1. Is there at least one member of the venture management team qualified to lead the team to undertake the necessary work?			
2. Is there an appropriate management team to undertake the work that has to be done?			
3. Is there an opportunity to bring in additional management either from the parent organization or outside directors?			
4. Is there an appropriate group of professionals in the existing organization or outside advisors?			
5. Does the venture management team have the ability and expertise to leverage scarce resources?			

Technological Viability

Evaluate the technological viability in relation to the following criteria:	Inadequate	Similar to competitors	Better than competitors	Excellent	Uncertain
1. Assess the feasibility and viability of technological development and achieving the specified goals and objectives.					
2. Compare the proposed development program with existing technologies (or with possible competing and future technologies).					
3. Evaluate the organization's existing technological achievements.					

Table 6.1 (continued)

Resources

Evaluate resources in relation to the following criteria:	Inadequate	Similar to competitors	Better than competitors	Excellent	Uncertain
1. Evaluate the adequacy of the organization's budget in the context of the potential new venture.					
2. Evaluate the possibility of raising additional funds to carry out the project, as well as the potential sources of funding available for the new venture.					
3. Evaluate the adequacy of the facilities required in relation to the availability of space for the new venture.					

Commercialization

Evaluate the commercialization in relation to the following criteria:	Inadequate	Similar to competitors	Better than competitors	Excellent	Uncertain
1. Evaluate the proposed commercialization schedule in relation to:					
a. R&D					
b. Proprietary protection					
c. Human resources					
d. Marketing					
e. Manufacturing					
f. Potential regulatory requirements.					
2. Assess the organization's ability to successfully compete in the market.					
3. Assess the organization's channels of distribution.					
4. Assess the organization's customer service philosophy.					
5. Assess the organization's capabilities in terms of:					
• financial control					
• management					
• strategic planning.					
6. Assess the feasibility of the organization's commercialization.					

The corporate entrepreneurial activity needs individuals who give unbiased advice and are relatively unconcerned about the parent company's internal politics. Finding such people is a challenge in most organizations. The secret to engaging the right people is to determine the skills and knowledge needed for corporate venturing. Corporate entrepreneurial activities often use outside advisors. These individuals are separate from the more formal board of advisors. Advisors should be interviewed just as if they were being hired for a permanent position with references checked.

When building a corporate entrepreneurial team, there can be a particular problem in determining compensation levels that are different from the standard compensation package offered. Issues most often occur if the parent company has corporate managers holding the most senior roles in the corporate venture who lead the venture in the usual manner of the corporate culture and control. Realizing that a new culture and environment is needed can be the first challenge to the company's culture and organization.

Companies such as Walmart, General Mills, Intel and United Parcel Service have invested millions of dollars in their venturing projects. One challenge is how to make early-stage financing decisions in corporate entrepreneurial ventures. If organizations like Cisco Systems, Genentech and Yahoo! were evaluated in their infancies on the basis of near-term earnings of a large corporation, they might never have become the businesses they are today.[1] A corporate entrepreneur recognizes the potential impact on the parent company's core business, has the drive and ability to influence any actions needed and creates, establishes and meets realistic milestones. The corporate entrepreneur needs to be an innovator with concern for the long-term viability of the new venture.

The best managers in an existing business are not necessarily the best for a new corporate venture. These managers often are more committed to preserving corporate traditions rather than challenge them. They often do not have the experience and ability needed for starting a new venture.

There may be, however, more corporate entrepreneurial individuals in the parent company than the management team realizes. Organizations can undertake the challenge of developing their internal executives and fostering an entrepreneurial culture. Companies such as Chevron

Corporation, United Airlines, Ford Motors and Xerox selected their corporate entrepreneurial leaders from internal ranks. A corporate entrepreneur needs to identify a core group of people who understand the business. This can be done using the following questions:

- Do we have a corporate entrepreneur who has the competencies and ability to lead the new venture?
- Do the existing advisors or board members have the expertise and knowledge to bring the corporate entrepreneurial venture to the next stage of its life cycle?
- Do we have a team of people who have the drive, motivation and experience to be part of this new corporate entrepreneurial venture?
- Is there evidence to suggest that the corporate entrepreneur and his team can effectively work together to achieve 'synergy'?

Corporate entrepreneurial team roles

One important factor is that the corporate venturing team can make decisions quickly. Corporate entrepreneurship takes many roles:

- Venture CEO. The corporate entrepreneur who is responsible for the overall development and advancement of the project.
- Technical innovator. The individual who is responsible for the major technical innovation, such as Art Fry, who developed 3M's Post-it Note.
- Product or service champion. All individuals who contribute to the project by promoting its development and advancement through all the key stages up to its implementation.
- Resource allocator. The individual who helps the venture obtain the necessary human and non-human resources.

Key characteristics of the corporate entrepreneurial leader

The corporate venturing leader needs to have the following characteristics:

- high energy level, drive and enthusiasm
- ability to attract, select and motivate the right people

- charisma to lead the venture and the team internally and externally
- resourcefulness
- excellent communication skills
- ability to sell the project internally and externally.

The leader needs to manage the expectations of:

- senior members of the parent company
- new corporate entrepreneurial venture managers and their team
- members of the organization at large
- all members associated with the new corporate entrepreneurial venture.

The corporate entrepreneur leading the new venture needs to:

- support and protect the team
- tolerate mistakes
- lead and advise management
- take moderate risks
- share the vision
- delegate to those closest to the problem
- tolerate internal competition
- stimulate innovation and creativity
- actively search for ideas
- tolerate disorder
- encourage experimentation and tests
- trust management and the team
- tolerate ambiguity
- drive and motivate the team.

The corporate entrepreneur needs to obtain appropriate support and collaboration and utilize resources, while acting in the best interest of both the new corporate venture and the overall organization. The team must have an entrepreneurial mindset, with each individual's activities properly integrated to achieve the goals and objectives.

Survival guidelines for corporate entrepreneurs

The following are some guidelines that have been followed by successful corporate entrepreneurs:

- Only pursue ideas where the potential reward justifies the potential risk.
- Request feedback at each stage of development.
- Identify an executive champion and other key alliances.
- Become your most objective and rigorous critic.
- Recognize your core competencies and utilize them to compensate for potential weaknesses.
- Avoid unnecessary publicity from the internal organization and the external media.
- Recognize and adapt to the life cycle stage of the corporate entrepreneurial venture.
- Ensure that new venture policies and procedures are developed and supported by the CEO.
- Lead by example, providing the leadership and the management for the venture.

Venture life cycle and selection of the corporate entrepreneurial team

At each stage of the corporate entrepreneurial venture's life cycle, there may be a need to change the team and even the corporate entrepreneur leading the team. Some team members will want to develop the corporate entrepreneurial venture through the main stages; others will see it as an opportunity for promotion within the parent organization; others will want to start additional new corporate entrepreneurial ventures; and others will want to go back to their previous position. Each stage of the process requires different skills and experience.

- *Conception and development.* At this stage, the corporate entrepreneur needs to demonstrate drive, motivation, perseverance, resourcefulness, charisma and the ability to communicate the opportunity to the team. This leader needs to be innovative, focused, and believe in the idea and the opportunities it can create and have the needed energy to complete the task.
- *Commercialization.* The corporate entrepreneur needs to demonstrate enthusiasm, desire and competence and be action orientated.
- *Growth and development.* Innovation and creativity are needed by the corporate entrepreneur to ensure further growth and development of the new venture.
- *Performance.* Since the corporate entrepreneurial venture has

been launched and maintained its position in the market, the corporate entrepreneur needs to develop the innovation to maintain its market position.

Companies such as Intel and Boeing invest millions in their corporate venturing group, with the goal of increasing their investment over time.

The corporate entrepreneur should lead the team by:

- developing effective problem-solving techniques
- piloting the methods (that is, identifying what needs to be changed)
- doing what it takes (that is, dedication and commitment)
- demonstrating clarity about what needs to be done
- encouraging participative decision making
- knowing the venture project
- keeping focused on the vision
- fostering teamwork.

Internal politics

Politics is inevitable in the work environment. Organizations consist of individuals and groups that bring their own interests, desires, wants, expectations and needs to the workplace, which result in a diversity of interests in which the politics occur. Relationships, norms, processes, performance and outcomes are significantly affected and influenced by organizational politics because they are all integrated into the organizational culture and management system.

Politics is a natural and expected characteristic of organizations. It may be precipitated by a combination of individual and contextual factors and is not necessarily viewed as self-serving.[2] Compensation, terms and conditions of employment, career advancement and progression are management systems that align the organizational and the employee interests. Individuals continue to act politically within the organization's political boundary and strive to improve their own benefits and satisfaction. The political capability of an organization is dependent upon its political resources in terms of influence bases. To ensure future political capability, the organization can attempt to expand or consolidate these bases. Table 6.2 summarizes the positive

Table 6.2   Positive and negative consequences of individual and organizational uses of political behavior

Positive	Negative
Individual	Individual
• Inspire confidence, trust and sincere behavioral attributes	• Frustration, de-motivation, dissatisfaction
• Increased assertiveness	• Low morale and loss of confidence
• Reduced anxiety and stress	• Increased anxiety and stress
• Improved position and influence	• Loss of position and influence
• Career advancement and progression	• Damaged reputation
Organizational	Organizational
• Support for desirable policies and procedures	• Negative manipulation and game-playing
• Contribute to organizational effectiveness	• Restrain organizational effectiveness
• Implement legitimate decisions	• Unethical decision making and use of resources
• Improve decision-making strategy	• Inhibit communication by increasing barriers
• Develop approaches for effective conflict resolution	• Inhibit goal attainment that will lead to conflict
• Create an environment that is adaptable to change	• Reduce flexibility and adaptability
• Manage resistance to change	• Block organizational change

and negative consequences of individual and organizational uses of political behavior.

Internal politics refers to the manner in which influence is distributed throughout the organization. Any level of change has the potential to modify the balance of power. The uncertainty created by change creates ambiguity, which increases the probability of political activity as individuals attempt to control their environment. In most companies, political influence is usually at the top of the organization.

To address this, important questions for corporate entrepreneurs include: who can underestimate the value of your idea? Who in the organization has the influence to inhibit an idea from being developed? Who has the final word on whether to embrace a new corporate entrepreneurial opportunity? To implement and develop corporate entrepreneurship, an innovative corporate entrepreneur must attempt to motivate and influence the key stakeholders. Failure to identify core stakeholders and effectively bring them on board can severely block the corporate entrepreneurship process and could potentially eliminate it altogether.

One popular method for attracting and aligning key stakeholders from top management for the corporate entrepreneurship is through 'stinging.' This method is often used by corporate entrepreneurs who need the support at the top to proceed. 'Stinging' involves carefully approaching top management individuals with a corporate venturing activity to determine their level of potential support. In this way, the corporate entrepreneur acts as the bee, treating top management as the hive and 'stinging' those members most likely to support the new idea before rolling it out to all top management members. Finding these internal, upper level champions is crucial for promoting the new idea in its initial stages. Starting in the 1980s, Goldman Sachs approached corporate entrepreneurship using a 'stinging' method with high level champions. This is the way Goldman Sachs successfully introduced and implemented its entrance into junk bonds and investment banking on a global scale.

Political problems can deter the corporate venturing process. Obstacles that have political ramifications that can inhibit the corporate venturing process include:

• Lack of adequate time and support to engage in corporate venturing.
• No compensation and reward system in place.
• Failure of corporate entrepreneurs to demonstrate the potential return on investment.
• Lack of adequate investment from the parent company.
• Inappropriate organizational structure in place that focuses on an autocratic style of management.
• Resistance from the company for the new corporate venturing concept or idea, which can result in limited interest or concern.
• Environment of fear, which constrains innovation and creativity throughout the organization.

Overcoming the obstacles

Each of these obstacles and negative implications results from management practices and internal organizational factors. In order to manage and overcome these, the corporate entrepreneur needs to influence and persuade the necessary individuals on the potential benefits of the corporate venturing activity. To gain support, the corporate entrepreneur needs to gain legitimacy, have access to the required human and non-human resources and be able to influence individuals at all levels of the organization.

Gaining legitimacy

The newer the market and idea, the more significant is the issue of legitimacy as there is no history or track record. From the beginning, corporate entrepreneurship needs to create a positive notion of capability and legitimacy. The basic and most influential tactic for gaining legitimacy is using personal and independent external advisors/ consultants to demonstrate the viability and credibility of the venturing activity. This is validated when the corporate entrepreneur has led success in developing new initiatives. Internal support from employees with a proven track record can add legitimacy to the project.

Human and non-human resource requirements

A new corporate venturing activity needs an adequate supply of both human and non-human resources to progress and develop. The corporate entrepreneur needs to determine if individuals with the required skills exist internally within the company or if there is a need to recruit key people externally. Non-human resources include funding, equipment, technology, access to production and service systems. The corporate entrepreneur usually faces constraints in the amount of resources that are available.

It is important that the corporate entrepreneur does not assume that the only way to receive needed resources is to deplete the resources from another department or project. This zero sum mindset often turns politics and competition into destructive conflict. Remember that one of the most valuable attributes of a corporate entrepreneur is his or her ability to innovate and create wealth – a positive sum game.

Overcoming resistance

Corporate venturing activities are often triggered by the need to respond to new challenges or opportunities occurring in the external environment. One frustration for corporate entrepreneurs is the

Table 6.3   Sources of resistance

Individual resistance	Organizational resistance
• Self-interest, for example, loss of influence, loss of freedom or loss of status associated with current position • Fear of the unknown • Reluctance and resentment • Lack of understanding and trust about the new venture • Risk and uncertainty associated with new venture activity • Different goals and objectives compared to the new venture • Feel the new venture is disturbing the status quo	• Organizational culture • Focus on maintaining stability • Failure to invest in additional resources required for the new venture • Inadequate financial resources • Threats to current power and/or influence • Too much competition for the new venture to adequately survive • Disturbs and threatens the current systems in place

resistance that occurs for no apparent reason. As indicated in Table 6.3, there are a number of reasons associated with resistance including self-interest, lack of understanding and trust, risk and uncertainty, and different goals and objectives. To effectively manage the implementation process, corporate entrepreneurs need to be aware of the reasons for resistance and be prepared to use techniques for obtaining cooperation (Box 6.1).

BOX 6.1   TECHNIQUES FOR OBTAINING COOPERATION

- Gain senior management support for the new venture activity.
- Educate all those about the benefits of the new venture by ensuring that all research has been carried out to provide accurate information.
- Communication with all those affected by the new venture.
- Participation from those individuals that are innovative and creative and can help bring the venture to fruition.
- Create opportunities for people to demonstrate their skills and competence.
- Build support networks inside and outside the organization.

Political strategy

Political strategies are specific tactics used to increase and effectively use influence. The political tactics needed to obtain resources, achieve agreement, and support and overcome potential barriers and resistance differ by organization. There are a number of tactics available to the corporate entrepreneur to deal with these problems.

It is best for the corporate entrepreneur not to ignore resistance but to diagnose the reasons for it and to design strategies to gain acceptance before officially announcing the new idea. One political strategy for overcoming the organizational resistance that inhibits the corporate venturing process has the following steps:

1. Clarify the short-, medium- and long-term goals and objectives of the corporate venturing activity. By clearly stating the core objectives, the corporate entrepreneur can identify who internally and externally would be affected by the new venture as well as who would be required to contribute.
2. Identify the potential political obstacles that would inhibit the corporate venture development. The corporate entrepreneur must review the various interest groups and identify the existing level of support, the opposition and their potential actions.
3. Identify individuals and groups that are neutral to the new venture's success. It is important to align these individuals and groups rather than risk them becoming opponents of the new venture.
4. Anticipate possible responses from individuals and groups. It is important that the corporate entrepreneur needs to be prepared for and able to manage a range of diverse responses and reactions from each individual and group. The corporate entrepreneur needs to be flexible and adjust the political strategy according to the anticipated response from specific individuals and groups.
5. Formulate a political strategy. The corporate entrepreneur needs to keep the process as straightforward as possible by focusing on key alliances and opponents.
6. Monitor and evaluate the progress of the political strategy. The corporate entrepreneur needs to monitor and evaluate the political strategy, identify any deviations and take appropriate corrective action.

Politics

Internal politics and the desire for control can significantly inhibit innovation and set the organization on the road to failure. This happens when the organizational structure and culture are valued over corporate venturing. Internal politics can make it very difficult for a culture of corporate entrepreneurship to flourish.

Microsoft cannot foster innovation if it threatens its political power and control. Frequently, larger software companies are seen in the continuous innovation camp but rarely as creators of discontinuous innovation. In more rigid, less adaptive cultures where resistance is the norm, there is a preference to wait until there is more clarity and less risk before engaging in corporate venturing activities. Resistant cultures place a premium on avoiding mistakes and leaning toward safe options.

A company that does not value managers and employees who are creative inhibits corporate entrepreneurship development. The big risk of this type of culture is that the organization can underestimate competitors and overestimate its own progression.

When these companies encounter rapidly changing business environments, the failure to move from the traditional ways can result in significant losses. The traditional mechanistic management practices designed and developed to manage large corporations are not conducive to corporate entrepreneurship as indicated in Table 6.4. In most cases, organizational strategies, systems, structures, rules, regulations, policies and procedures are designed and developed to achieve organizational goals and objectives rather than engage in corporate venturing activities.

General Motors, IBM and Sears are examples of companies whose traditional bureaucracies did not adequately respond to the fundamental changes in their markets. The cultures and behaviors were not suited to achieve market success and, as a result, these companies struggled during this time. Companies like Amazon.com, Google, Dell Computer, Intel, Nokia and 3M rapidly adapt and adjust to the needs of the environment. They are practitioners of corporate venturing and innovation and have the willingness to take the necessary risks to create new products, new businesses and new industries.

Table 6.4 Traditional management practices that inhibit corporate entrepreneurial activities

Traditional management practices	Negative implications
Rigidly defined rules, regulations and procedures	Innovation and creativity inhibited
Mechanistic organizational structure in place	Corporate entrepreneurial activities are limited and diverse
Control system with limited delegation of autonomy and authority	Opportunities to be corporate entrepreneurs are limited and diverse
Avoid any risk and uncertainty to the existing organization	Fear of change and any threat to the existing organization causes potential opportunities to be not recognized or considered
Future decisions based on past performance	Failure to recognize market changes leading to inaccurate decisions
Limited compensation and reward system	Limited motivation and incentives to be innovative
Standard promotion system in place based on years of service and compatibility to organizational ethos	Lack of opportunity for motivated corporate entrepreneurs to add value

In particular, Intel took a corporate venturing risk with its entrance into the Japanese market where it came up against entrenched government-supported competitors. Intel was not a household name in Japan where branding is a key ingredient for attracting Japanese consumers. Intel internally came up with a new branding strategy of aligning itself with the Walt Disney theme park and cartoon characters in Japan. Intel discovered that most electronic purchases in Japan were made by women and that Japanese women loved Disney characters.

Political tactics for corporate entrepreneurs to increase their influence

Corporate entrepreneurs use political tactics to increase their influence by increasing the validity and credibility of a new corporate venturing activity. This can be accomplished by managing and controlling risk and uncertainty, becoming invaluable to the organization, leading and

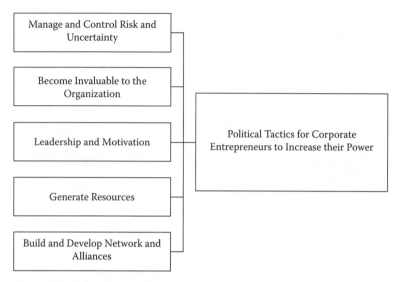

Figure 6.1   Political tactics for increasing power in an organization

motivating individuals, generating appropriate resources, and building and developing networks and alliances (Figure 6.1).

- Manage and control risk and uncertainty: corporate entrepreneurs who can manage risk and reduce uncertainty for the organization, increase influence and become leaders.
- Become invaluable to the organization: develop valuable core competencies (knowledge, skill and abilities).
- Leadership and motivation: corporate entrepreneurs can lead and control the organization's activities if they have the right mindset to motivate individuals and gain support.
- Generate resources: corporate entrepreneurs need to recruit, select and retain skilled people or attract appropriate financing and investment.
- Build and develop networks and alliances: develop mutually beneficial relations inside and outside the organization.

Political tactics for corporate entrepreneurs to exercise influence

It is important for corporate entrepreneurs to think in terms of short- and long-term goals and objectives for the new venture project. As

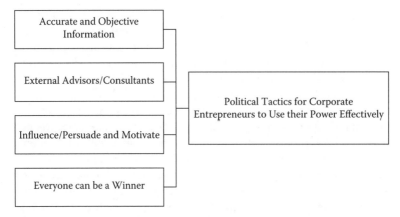

Figure 6.2   Political tactics for corporate venturers to exercise power

indicated in Figure 6.2, politically skilled corporate entrepreneurs have an ability to utilize the five political tactics for increasing influence as well as an appreciation for the political tactics to exercise influence.

- Accurate and objective information: all information needs be accurate and objective in order to gain trust and integrity within the organization.
- External advisors/consultants: bring in an expert or group of experts who can objectively support the corporate entrepreneurial proposal as this increases its credibility.
- Influence/persuade and motivate: use political tactics to influence, persuade and motivate the behavior of all those involved in the decision-making process.

Everyone can be a winner: emphasize the benefits of the new corporate entrepreneurial opportunity to everyone whose support is needed as well by highlighting the personal benefits from providing that support.

Summary

Corporate entrepreneurs can become so focused and committed to the corporate venturing activity that they neglect its context. Politics exist in every organization to some extent and need to be managed as effectively as possible. In managing internal politics, the corporate entrepreneur needs to inform and use key supporters, alliances and networks inside and outside the parent organization. Recognizing the importance of internal politics and the development of political tactics is an important aspect of corporate entrepreneurship. The influence of managers can inhibit even the most opportunistic corporate venture or alternatively it can ensure its progression and success. Corporate entrepreneurial failures are frequently due to the difficulty in gaining legitimacy, inadequate human and non-human resources requirements and inability to overcome resistance. The corporate entrepreneur needs to devote appropriate time and effort to managing and overcoming any objections from the internal politics. Corporate entrepreneurs need to determine the core issues and problems, identify their key supporters and recognize and manage problematic individuals. They should cautiously move forward while developing political tactics that will manage and solve the problems through supporters and networks inside and outside the organization.

NOTES
1 James Clayton, Bradley Gambill and Douglas Harned, 'The curse of too much capital: building new businesses in large corporations,' *The McKinsey Quarterly*, **3**, 1999, 48–59.
2 D.A. Buchanan, 'You stab my back, I'll stab yours: management experience and perceptions of organization political behavior,' *British Journal of Management*, **19**, 2008, 49–64.

Online source

http://www.textron.com/about/company/history.php.

7 Controlling and compensating corporate venturing

Scenario: Trojan Technologies

It all began in 1976, when a young entrepreneur named Hank Vander Laan, and his partners, bought Trojan Metal Products Limited – a small company located in London, Ontario, Canada.

Although fabricating metal toolboxes was Trojan Metal Products' mainstay, what caught Vander Laan's eye were the patent rights it held on a small ultraviolet (UV) treatment unit for homeowners to use to purify their drinking water. He was aware of the benefits of UV as a safer, more environmentally friendly alternative to chemical water treatment, and envisioned the potential for large-scale applications. Soon thereafter, development commenced on a commercially viable UV disinfection system for municipal wastewater treatment. The journey to transform the fledgling metal fabricator into a dynamic global company capable of solving complex water problems had begun.

In 1983, the business was reorganized to form Trojan Technologies Inc. Also, it was around this time that the company was awarded its first municipal wastewater project in Tillsonburg, Ontario, Canada.

Fueled by early success, the company accelerated its investment in research and development (R&D), and began developing a full suite of UV systems for municipal wastewater, industrial applications and small, residential applications.

The company experienced rapid growth throughout the 1980s and 1990s, particularly in the municipal wastewater sector. During this time, it was proud to pioneer many innovations that revolutionized municipal wastewater treatment. Over the course of the two decades, it installed thousands of systems in over 25 countries.

By 1993, it was honored as one of the world leaders in UV disinfection technology. However, to achieve the next level of growth, access to more capital was required. That same year, it launched a successful initial public offering and became a publicly traded company, listed on the Toronto Stock Exchange.

This initial and subsequent infusion of investor capital allowed it to expand production facilities, streamline manufacturing and diversify beyond municipal wastewater disinfection and into municipal drinking water treatment. The TrojanUVSwift™ immediately caught the attention of municipalities everywhere and by 2002, it had won important contracts to supply equipment to three large UV drinking water plants (Seattle, Washington; Victoria, British Columbia and Rotterdam, the Netherlands).

A series of strategic acquisitions allowed the company to continue diversification into other important markets.

Recognizing the tremendous potential of the emerging field of environmental contaminant treatment (ECT), Advanced Ultraviolet Solutions (based in Tucson, Arizona) was acquired in 2001. This gave the company access to a process called UV-oxidation – an advanced water treatment method that eliminates harmful chemical contaminants, including pesticides and herbicides, while also inactivating microorganisms, such as *Escherichia coli*, *Cryptosporidium* and *Giardia*.

In the industrial UV sector, several acquisitions and alliances in Europe and North America helped broaden distribution, product line and capabilities. From 2001 to 2003, a period of relatively soft growth for the industry as a whole, Trojan Technologies Inc. was able to expand industrial sales by nearly 350 percent. Its residential UV sector was also beginning to flourish.

In 2004, US Peroxide LLC was acquired. It is North America's largest direct supplier of hydrogen peroxide (H_2O_2) for environmental service applications. This helped enable an integrated ECT product offering (H_2O_2 is the oxidant used in the UV-oxidation process).

It was also at this time that their municipal UV business identity was rebranded to TrojanUV, which meant that all municipal wastewater and drinking water disinfection and ECT systems were provided by TrojanUV.

Near the end of 2004, Trojan joined Danaher Corporation (DHR: NYSE). Danaher was a Fortune 200, global science and technology leader and part of their environmental segment and water quality group.

In 2005, Aquafine Corporation was acquired. Established in 1949, it had grown to become a leader and product innovator in water treatment for the industrial and commercial market sectors. All of Trojan Technologies' industrial UV business was integrated into Aquafine.

In 2008, R-Can Environmental Inc. – a leading manufacturer of residential water treatment/disinfection systems – was acquired. All of Trojan Technologies' residential UV was then merged and integrated, and R-Can was reorganized to form VIQUA. Going forward, all residential UV solutions were provided by them.

Trojan Technologies Inc. had built a solid foundation and culture upon which new and eco-efficient water treatment technologies could be discovered, conceived and propelled. Its group of businesses was poised to diversify outside the UV industry.

In 2010, Trojan Technologies unveiled the Trojan Marinex division. Its focus is solely on the marine industry and providing ballast water treatment (BWT) solutions. Trojan Marinex offers a suite of BWT systems that provide filtration plus UV in a single, compact unit.

In 2011, OpenCEL was acquired and became a division of Trojan Technologies. Its focused pulse cell lysis technology applies high frequency electronic pulses to rupture cell membranes, releasing soluble material that can more readily be reduced and converted to energy.

In 2012, Salsnes Filter was acquired. Its filter systems are installed around the world in a variety of applications within municipal wastewater treatment plants and in challenging industrial solids separation applications. As its group of businesses continues to grow, so too does its history. The company believes that it is of the utmost importance to document their history so that you can see where they began, where they've been and where they're going.

Evaluating the corporate entrepreneurial team's performance

Evaluating performance focuses on how close the corporate entrepreneurial team achieves its goals and objectives. While the corporate venture starts with clearly defined goals and objectives, it needs to be flexible.

Cisco followed an unconventional form of corporate venturing known as 'external R&D.' The company developed a tight formula for evaluating, acquiring and integrating start-ups and growing technology firms, acquiring more than 65 start-ups in the last decade. The performance of a single venture should not inhibit the parent organization as the new corporate venture directly influences the cash flow and profit of the parent.

Evaluation criteria for the corporate entrepreneurial team

It is not appropriate to evaluate a new corporate venture using the traditional performance criteria of the parent company. Evaluation criteria need to be focused on timely completion of events at a reasonable cost, with quality standards being maintained. There also needs to be evidence of teamwork, collaboration and commitment.

One approach to establishing appropriate evaluation criteria is:

- *Identify what to evaluate.* All evaluations need to be undertaken with a clear, objective and consistent approach. All key aspects need to establish an appropriate and consistent evaluation strategy for comparative purposes.
- *Clearly define the desired standards of performance.* These need to be realistic and clearly communicated to all involved. Standards can be measured at intervals as well as on completion to ensure that events have been completed within a reasonable timeframe and at a reasonable cost.
- *Assess and evaluate actual standards of performance.* Assessment needs to be carried out within a timeframe based on the quality of alternative courses of action.
- *Compare the desired standard of performance with the actual standard of performance.* If there are acceptable differences

between the actual and the desired performance, then the evaluation and control process has worked.

- *Appropriate courses of action need to be undertaken if any deviations are identified.* If deviations are unacceptable, then action must be undertaken quickly.

While an effective control system does not guarantee organizational success, it does contribute toward it. Corporate entrepreneurship needs a control system that is developed and implemented based on the long-term goals and objectives of the organization. Each venture control should:

1. be easy to understand and apply to the new venture
2. assess and evaluate all important venture activities
3. be undertaken within an appropriate timeframe
4. be short term, medium term and long term
5. quickly and comprehensively identify any deviations
6. be adapted to help the new venture excel.

The control system needs to be flexible while evaluating the performance of the corporate entrepreneurs and their venture.

Compensating corporate entrepreneurs

Corporate entrepreneur compensation and incentive practices vary greatly. At Nokia, there are no financial incentives. At DCA Food Industries Inc., 20 percent of profits go to the corporate venture management team. Tektronix offers salary-related milestone awards. At 3M, all individuals involved in the new corporate entrepreneurial venture will have changes in their employment and compensation as a function of the product sales growth achieved. Because new product sponsorship is the responsibility of management, 3M has special compensation incentives for those managers.

The compensation program of the corporate entrepreneur leading the venture needs to have an incentive to motivate individuals to achieve desirable performance and be related to the returns to the organization. The financial incentive package will also help attract and retain the appropriate team. The following are aspects that need to be considered in developing an appropriate compensation plan:

- emphasize long-term performance
- customize specifically for the new venture
- tailor to individuals achieving and excelling performance outcomes
- emphasize individual performance with incentives for teamwork
- merit and incentive based
- significant financial reward over a certain timeframe
- based on external equity.

Compensation plans are important to retain innovative and creative people; these incentives need to be motivational. Individual incentives need to be balanced with group incentives to encourage individuals to work on their own initiative as well as being part of a team. While it is more challenging to link compensation to collective performance of a corporate entrepreneurial venture, it can be done by basing salary increases on the attainment of milestones or giving corporate entrepreneurs a share in the ownership or performance of the corporate venture. These can take the form of large bonuses or stock options that vest over a period of time.

The compensation package is especially important in attracting individuals in the following circumstances:

- If an internal person is being encouraged to leave a major project to join the new corporate venturing team.
- If an external person is being encouraged to leave an existing high-profile position to join the new corporate venturing team.
- If financial incentives are a major motivating factor for the internal or external individual to take the position in the corporate venture.
- In terms of balancing the risk and reward factors associated with leaving a more secure position to take a position in the corporate venture.
- As a demonstration of appreciation for the hard work and commitment of the corporate venturing team.

If the corporate entrepreneur and the team are not adequately compensated, the parent company is essentially encouraging them to leave the organization. If the company develops a compensation plan that is weighted toward unrealistic targets, it will frustrate employees. While it is easy to reward success, according to Xerox, it is more important to reward failure. Xerox does not judge people by results, but by the quality of their efforts.

While Hewlett-Packard and Microsoft compete for software engineers, each company demonstrates a different corporate culture, which is reinforced in their compensation systems.[1] This also applies to Toyota and Toshiba, which have the same national culture but different organizational cultures, and different compensation and reward systems.[2] From a strategic perspective, organizations need to structure compensation and reward systems that develop a corporate entrepreneurial culture.

Components of a compensation and incentive system

The following compensation and incentive components can help develop a compensation plan that attracts and retains corporate entrepreneurs who will successfully contribute to the development of the new ventures.

- *Equity*. Part ownership interest in the new corporate entrepreneurial venture or parent company in the form of common stock or preferred stock.
- *Bonuses*. Money linked to individual or group performance achievements such as sales, profits and return on investments. These amounts can be fixed, variable or discretionary.
- *Salary increases*. Applied in the same way to a new corporate entrepreneurial venture as the existing corporation.
- *Career progression and advancement*. As opportunities emerge, those who make the greatest contribution to the new corporate entrepreneurial venture should be recognized and given the chance to apply for a more advanced position.
- *Recognition and rewards*. Non-financial incentives can be as valuable to many corporate entrepreneurs as financial incentives. Individuals recognized for their contribution through recognition ceremonies and awards (that can be financial, which occurs at Du Pont), peer recognition, employee of the month or sponsorship of sabbaticals. These incentives need to be consistent with the organizational culture and equitable to all who make certain achievements and contributions to the new venture.

Compensation and incentive components for new success

Table 7.1 identifies some compensation and incentives that can contribute to the success of the corporate entrepreneurial venture.

Some creative approaches to compensating and rewarding corporate entrepreneurial behavior include:

- Employees put a percentage of their salary at risk and then can either lose it, double it or triple it based on team performance.
- Personalized 'innovator' jackets, shirts and leather folders are given to employees who make entrepreneurial contributions.
- When a new idea is accepted by the company, the CEO awards shares of stock to the employee.
- Employees are given $500 to spend on an innovative idea that relates to their job.
- A company rents out a major sports stadium, fills the stands with employees, families and friends and then has innovation champions run onto the field as their name and achievement appears on the scoreboard.
- A company sets a target and then 30 percent of incremental earnings above that target are placed into a bonus pool that is paid out based on each employee's performance rating.
- Small cash awards are given to employees who try something new and fail, and the best failure of the quarter receives a larger sum.
- Some companies have point systems where employees receive differing amounts of points for different categories of innovation contributions. Points are redeemable for computers, merchandise, free day care, tuition reimbursement and other types of rewards.
- A parking spot is reserved for the 'innovator of the month.'
- Team members working on a major innovation are awarded shares of zero value at project outset, and as milestones are achieved (on time), predetermined values are added to the shares. Milestones not achieved lead to a decline in share value.
- Another company ties cash awards for employees to a portfolio of innovation activities produced over time, including ideas generated, patents applied for, prototypes developed and so forth.
- Employees receive recognition for innovative suggestions, and then a drawing is held at the end of the year for all accepted suggestions, with the winner receiving a sizeable financial reward.

Table 7.1   Compensation and incentive factors for corporate entrepreneurship

Corporate entrepreneurship success factors	Compensation and incentive factors that influence satisfaction
Satisfaction with the compensation and incentives offered	• Purchasing power: based on the standard of living • Fairness: a personalized evaluation of what is seen as appropriate commensurate with ability, contribution and effort • Equitable: in terms of internal and external comparisons • Expectation and value: where the rewards meet expectations as to their value and are commensurate with the effort and skill needed to achieve them • Balanced: between intrinsic and extrinsic rewards • Total package: depends on the overall mix of compensation and incentives offered
Drive, motivation and commitment among CEO, venture management and the team	• Competitive earning opportunities • Transparency and equity in compensation and incentives • Equitable and competitive plan in relation to parent company and external organizations • Individual compensation and incentive plans • Financial and non-financial incentives offered
Effective teamwork and synergy	• Teamwork incentive plans • Equity and fairness for all team members and their contributions • Effective composition of team members • Team recognition
Corporate and new venture	• Parent company support for the new venture and recognition and respect for the differences between them • Providing a balance between the risks taken and rewards offered
Recognizing the importance of the external environment	• Team flexibility and adaptability to external environmental factors • Individual and group autonomy to achieve desirable results in light of change

- One company has a 'frequent innovator' program that works like an airline frequent flier program.
- 'Hero biographies' are written about an employee, her background and an innovation that she has championed. The stories are full of praise and a little humor.
- One company provides gift certificates within a day of an employee idea being implemented, and another takes employees to a 'treasure box' where they can choose from among a number of gifts.
- A company gives 15 percent of out-of-pocket savings achieved by the innovator's ideas in the first two years of use and, if the idea is for a product, 3 percent of first-year sales.
- The top-performing team in terms of innovation is sent to a resort for a week.
- A company gives a savings bond to the employee who raises the most challenging question in management meetings.
- One organization has $500 on-the-spot awards for anyone showing special initiative.
- Some companies have their own Olympics, rodeos, competitions, game shows, hit parades and murder mysteries in an attempt to recognize initiative and excellence.
- Others have praise and recognition boards, threshold performance clubs and Atta-person awards, and some allow innovators to appear in company advertisements.

There are some key lessons for corporations and their new ventures:

- The corporate venture needs to create an environment that the corporate culture supports and facilitates the new venture.
- New venture goals and objectives are different from corporate goals and objectives.
- New ventures can learn valuable lessons from the corporate venture as a way of identifying innovative opportunities for growth and development.
- Having the right people in the right place at the right time is critical to new venture success.
- It takes time, commitment and energy for the new venture to develop. It must be monitored and evaluated to measure its progress and recognize the need for changes or termination.
- Compensation and incentive practices should be fair and equitable in the context of the new venture's goals and objectives, culture and needs of management and their team.

Summary

This chapter has focused on a fundamental component of corporate entrepreneurial venturing – attracting, recruiting, selecting, evaluating and compensating the corporate entrepreneur and the team. The corporate entrepreneurial activity needs to attract talent and establish relationships with potential partners, advisors, consultants and customers. A corporate entrepreneur needs to be committed and enthusiastic and effectively manage, lead and integrate. The selection of a board of advisors adds support. Proper recruitment and selection procedures need to be established to ensure that potential internal and/or external innovative candidates are recruited and selected.

The corporate entrepreneurial activity needs to be monitored and evaluated by milestones that are based on the completion of tasks and whether desirable results are achieved. Continual evaluations are needed so that corrective action can be quickly taken. Appropriate compensation and incentive plans need to be in place. There should be both financial and non-financial compensation and incentive plans including equity, bonuses, salary increases, career progression and advancement, and recognition and rewards.

NOTES

1 Michael Beer, Rakesh Khurana and James Weber, 'Hewlett-Packard: culture in changing times,' *Harvard Business School Case*, Cambridge, MA, 5 February, 2004.

2 George Milkovich, Barry Gerhart and Jerry Newman, *Compensation* (9th edn), Boston, MA: McGraw-Hill/Irwin, 2008, p. 509.

Online sources

http://www.trojantechnologies.com/about/history/.
http://www.bloomberg.com/profiles/companies/TUV:CN-trojan-technologies-inc.

8 Implementing corporate venturing

Scenario: Tesla Motors

Tesla Motors was founded in 2003 by a group of engineers in Silicon Valley who wanted to prove that electric cars are better than gasoline-powered cars. With instant torque, incredible power and zero emissions, Tesla's products would be exceptional cars. Each new generation being increasingly affordable and, helping the company work toward its mission: to accelerate the world's transition to sustainable transport.

Tesla's engineers first designed a powertrain for a sports car built around an AC induction motor, patented in 1888 by Nikola Tesla, the inventor who inspired the company's name. The resulting Tesla Roadster was launched in 2008, setting a new standard for electric mobility. The company has sold approximately 2,500 Tesla Roadsters to customers in approximately 30 countries, predominately in North America and Europe.

In 2012, Tesla launched Model S, the world's first premium electric sedan. Built from the ground up to be 100 percent electric, Model S has redefined the very concept of a four-door car. With room for seven passengers and more than 64 cubic feet of storage, Model S provides the comfort and utility of a family sedan while achieving the acceleration of a sports car: 0 to 60 mph in about 5 seconds. Its flat battery pack is integrated into the chassis and sits below the occupant cabin, lending the car a low center of gravity that enables outstanding road holding and handling while driving 265 miles per charge. Model S was named Motor Trend's 2013 Car of the Year and achieved a five-star safety rating from the US National Highway Traffic Safety Administration.

In late 2014, Tesla CEO Elon Musk unveiled two dual motor all-wheel drive configurations of Model S that further improve the vehicle's handling and performance. The 85D features a high efficiency motor at the front and rear, giving the car unparalleled control of traction in all conditions. The P85D pairs a high efficiency front motor with a performance rear motor for supercar acceleration, achieving a 0 to 60 mph time of 3.2 seconds – the fastest four-door car ever made.

Now with more than 50,000 vehicles on the road worldwide, Tesla is preparing to launch Model X, a crossover vehicle that enters volume production in the latter half of 2016. Featuring exhilarating acceleration, falcon wing doors and room for three rows of seating, Model X defies categorization.

Tesla owners enjoy the benefit of charging at home so they never have to visit a gas station or spend a cent on gasoline. For long distance journeys, Tesla's Supercharger network provides convenient and free access to high speed charging, replenishing half a charge in as little as 20 minutes. Superchargers now connect popular routes in North America, Europe and the Asia Pacific.

Tesla's vehicles are produced at its factory in Fremont, California, previously home to New United Motor Manufacturing Inc., a joint venture between Toyota and General Motors. The Tesla factory has returned thousands of jobs to the area and is capable of producing 1,000 cars a week.

The company is expanding its manufacturing footprint into other areas, including Tilburg, the Netherlands, where it has an assembly facility, and Lathrop, California, where it has a specialized production plant. To reduce the costs of lithium ion battery packs, Tesla and key strategic partners including Panasonic have begun construction of a gigafactory in Nevada that will facilitate the production of a mass-market affordable vehicle, Model 3. By 2020, the gigafactory will produce more lithium ion cells than all of the world's combined output in 2013. The gigafactory will also produce battery packs intended for use in stationary storage, helping to improve robustness of the electrical grid, reduce energy costs for businesses and residences and provide a backup supply of power.

The company began customer deliveries of Model X in the third quarter of 2015. After its initial launch in the United States, Model X will be sold in all the markets where Model S is available, including Asia and Europe. The company has publicly announced its intent to develop a third generation electric vehicle, called Model 3. The company's vehicle, the Tesla Roadster, is the electric sports car. It can accelerate from o to 60 miles per hour in as little as 3.7 seconds and has a maximum speed of approximately 120 miles per hour. The Tesla Roadster also has a range of 245 miles on a single charge, as determined using the US Environmental Protection Agency's combined two-cycle city/highway test. Using the energy management technologies and manufacturing processes developed for the company's vehicle powertrain systems, it has developed stationary energy storage products for use in homes, commercial sites and utilities.

Models of corporate venturing

Corporate venturing is one strategy for improving corporate performance. Internal corporate venturing occurs when the new process or new business is created within the company's organizational domain. External corporate venturing involves strategic investments outside the company's organizational domain. Joint corporate venturing is a form of external corporate venturing that involves a co-investment with another parent organization that results in the creation of a new organization with both parent organizations continuing to exist.

There are five overall general business models of corporate venturing.

Model 1

Model 1, according to Andrew Campbell, highlights four different types of corporate entrepreneurial business ventures: (1) ecosystem venturing; (2) innovation venturing; (3) harvest venturing; and (4) private equity venturing.[1] Ecosystem venturing refers to promoting the vivacity of the business network (customers, suppliers, distributors and franchisees). Ecosystem venturing supports entrepreneurs in the specific business community through venture capital to improve prospects of existing businesses.[2] Value is created through the minority stakes in the invested firms.

The second type of venturing, innovation venturing, is the implementation of venture capital methods into existing functions such as R&D. This model is used to help stimulate activity by rewarding people based on the value created within an existing function.

The third type of business model is harvest venturing. This model seeks to generate cash from excess corporate resources through licensing or the sale of assets. Often, new businesses are created to fully utilize the excess resources.

Corporate private equity venturing, the fourth type, relates to company units that function as independent private equity groups to obtain financial returns.

Model 2

Model 2 identifies five types of linkages between corporate venturing and business strategy to explain how companies are venturing in ways to strategically benefit the existing company: (1) corporate venturing and business strategy are poorly linked or unrelated; (2) business strategy drives corporate venturing; (3) corporate venturing drives business strategy; (4) corporate venturing and business strategy are interdependent; and (5) corporate venturing as the business strategy.[3] Corporate venturing can be an internal corporate venturing whereby a new business is created within the domain of the existing company. A second type is external corporate venturing where the company is involved in creating a new business or growing a business outside the parent company's domain. Joint corporate venturing is the third category and refers to an external corporate venturing established by the existing business and another parent organization.

Model 3

Garud and Van den Ven's model for internal corporate venturing is trial-and-error learning.[4] This model is based on the observation that the internal corporate entrepreneurial process is filled with uncertainty and ambiguity. Uncertainty is defined as the incomplete information of the underlying relationship between means and ends. The assumption is that corporate entrepreneurs will continue with the plan when the associated outcomes are positive, and when the outcomes are negative, they will stop or change their course of action. This model argues that when the level of ambiguity is high and excess resources are available, corporate entrepreneurs are more likely to persist with a course of action despite negative consequences.

Innovative companies are less likely to penalize entrepreneurs in the early stages of the development process. It is more beneficial for the company to provide support through a trial-and-error process whereby the entrepreneur makes decisions based on what he believes will yield successful outcomes.

Ambiguity, on the other hand, implies incomplete information about which outcomes to pursue. When ambiguity comes into play and excess resources are available, entrepreneurs are likely to continue with a course of action despite facing negative outcomes.

Model 4

Since a company's foundation is its current business activities, corporate venturing is the introduction of a business model that is new to the company.[5]

In the company's operating core, where profits are generated in existing business activities, there is lower risk. In the business extension for growth, there is low to medium risk. Here, the company introduces new products or moves into new markets. Core ventures for renewal involve existing business activities but risk increases slightly from low to medium. As newness increases, so does the risk; therefore, the non-core venturing quadrant carries the most risk.

Based on the strategic pair analysis, the business activity and the business model, businesses should maintain core venturing capabilities as a defense against disruptive change. Instead of non-core ventures, it is important and practical for companies to focus on corporate venturing inside the existing business structure.

Model 5

Robert A. Burgelman lays out a process model for internal corporate venturing in major diversified firms.[6] In the process model for internal corporate venturing, there are three main elements: (1) definition and impetus; (2) strategic and structural context; and (3) managerial activities. As the core processes of internal corporate venturing, definition and impetus are the first step in the model process. The definition process includes the conceptualization and pre-venture stages of the development process. Moreover, the model involves expressing the technical and economic qualities of an internal corporate venturing project so that a project develops into an embryonic business organization. The linking processes are important in demonstrating that the newly developed concept is coupled to a market need. Product championing takes the linking process further and pushes it to the impetus process.

Support within the organization is then obtained through the impetus process because market interest is created and resources are mobilized. In the impetus process, a project transforms from a venture idea into its own business. Strategic forcing is the commercialization of the new product, which needs to be combined with efforts from strategic building. In this way, both a broader strategy and the implementation of the strategy are developed for the new business.

The second element of the internal corporate venturing process encompasses strategic context and structural context. Strategic context determination is the political process whereby managers of the corporate entrepreneurial business persuade corporate managers to alter the existing concept of strategy to include the new venture. The goal is to gain support from upper corporate management by showing them how the corporate entrepreneurial activity fits into the current strategy and has strategic benefits. Delineation is also an important factor that helps outline the new arenas into which the business development will lead the existing company. Structural context refers to the internal selection environment whereby corporate managers exert control over the internal corporate venturing process.

The third element of the internal corporate venturing process addresses the vital role middle level management plays. The process is a bottom-up approach, and managers must foster support and secure resources for new venturing strategically. Management championing the new corporate entrepreneurial activity must be adept at linking the new business venture with the corporate strategy.

Specific examples of corporate venturing

To better understand the way corporate venturing can work in an organization, four examples – 3M, Grameen Bank, Xerox and Google – are discussed.

3M

Creativity, risk, innovation and the spirit of entrepreneurship are words strongly associated with 3M (formerly Minnesota Mining and

Manufacturing). While some of their products are widely known, such as Post-It Notes and sandpaper products, others are found in medical equipment, dog food and Apple iPhones. In fact, to date, there are over 55,000 3M products in the market.[7] The company's secret to improving its existing products and bringing new products to market is its culture of innovation and corporate venturing. A few of its cultural characteristics are described below.

Fifteen percent rule

3M gives the right to its researchers to spend up to 15 percent of their work time pursuing whatever research idea interests them. The employees can use the time to travel to other labs and conferences, research and brainstorm, or tinker in the lab. According to Bill Coyne, 3M's head of R&D, the purpose of the 15 percent rule is that the 'system has some slack in it. If you have a good idea, and the commitment to squirrel away time to work on it, and the raw nerve to skirt your lab manager's expressed desires, then go for it.'[8]

Communication

The company encourages researchers to seek advice from outside their own labs. To encourage the flow of ideas within the company and foster a sense of community, managers try to bring people together through such semi-structured events as meetings, conferences, cross-functional teams, computer software and databases.

Genesis grants

This is a grant awarded to company scientists by their peers for research projects that might not otherwise receive funding in part due to the particular idea not fitting in with the division's business plans. The award is up to $100,000.[9]

Pacing Plus

This is a system that fast-tracks projects that have high potential to win in the market. The criteria and characteristics for the Pacing Plus program are to 'change the basis of competition in new or existing markets; offer large sales and profit potential, with attractive returns on investment; receive priority access to 3M resources; operate in an accelerated time frame; and employ the best available product commercialization processes.'[10] The Pacing Plus program is considered to be one of the most effective management tools used at 3M to encourage a project with high potential.

Goal

3M has instituted a corporate goal to generate 30 percent of revenue from new products introduced in the past five years. Referred to as a stretch target, this 30 percent goal has helped spark creativity within the entire company.

A final factor in 3M's success with corporate venturing is management's tolerance and acceptance of high risk. The company views failure as a learning opportunity, encouraging those who want to prove the practicality or impracticality of an idea.

Grameen Bank

The implementation of corporate venturing has at its core a dire need for resources and often in its most basic form. A bamboo stool-maker in Jobra, India, by the name of Sufia Khatun, was a struggling entrepreneur under the pressing restraints of high interest loans. In exchange for the loan, the local lender required her to sell the stools back to the organization at such a low price that she made only two cents profit per day as compared to her potential earnings of $1.25. This was a common occurrence in the city of Jobra, contributing to its debilitating poverty. This was noticed by an economics professor named Muhammad Yunus in 1974. Further investigation revealed that 47 local entrepreneurs like Khatun were caught in this cycle, yet had the potential to make considerably higher profits if relieved of the high interest debt. Yunus discovered that these entrepreneurs needed very little money to pay off the loans; Yunus found a group of informal backers willing to invest this money at more reasonable interest rates. All 47 loans were repaid and the entrepreneurs were able to earn higher profit margins and climb above the poverty level. This was the beginning of Grameen Bank headquartered in Bangladesh, India and the start of the microfinance and microcredit industry. Muhammad Yunus, the founder of the microcredit Grameen Bank, which was officially recognized by the Indian government in 1983, was the recipient of the Nobel Peace Prize. His objectives are to reach the poorest families and empower those entrepreneurs with the potential to earn wealth rather than loaning money to those with money and collateral. This allowed poverty-stricken families and less developed nations to create a higher level of living without having the valuable monetary resources.

The microcredit business model as practiced by Grameen Bank is based on a conjoint goal combining economic results with social initiatives. It focuses on providing financial loans to create entrepreneurs in the poorest sectors, particularly women living in rural areas. Yunus and Grameen Bank believe that obtaining loans at reasonable, repayable rates should be a basic right, accessible to those who need it the most. The loans are given in small increments (micro) with repayment schedules based on weekly amounts. There are no official documents protecting the repayment of the loans as they are based on the honor system (social responsibility of the group), with pay periods being extended if the recipients experience financial troubles.

Unlike conventional loans, these are based on simple interest rather than quarterly compounded interest rates with any excess profits (after costs are covered) being put back into the bank or used for local initiatives such as education for children and women in these rural areas, such as nutritional yogurt for the malnourished, bed nets to protect villagers from malaria spread by mosquitoes and information technology to leapfrog the rural areas into the twenty-first century. Due to its business practices, microcredit requires investors willing to earn smaller amounts of money but large social returns. Yunus and Grameen Bank have attracted large global firms like Danone, Intel and BASF as well as non-government organizations and governments from countries like Norway, Sweden and Germany to be investors backing these loans to provide entrepreneurial support in less developed areas.

Positive results have occurred as a result of these microcredit activities. Benefits include a 99 percent repayment rate and 58 percent of the borrowing families moving out of poverty. Grameen Bank has loaned $5.7 billion since its inception to over 6.6 million people, 97 percent of whom are women. The bank now has 2,226 branches serving over 71,000 villages. These entrepreneurs did indeed have enormous potential when the needed resources were available. As of December 2010, Yunus and Grameen Bank have been under close scrutiny by the Norwegian government and the Bangladeshi Prime Minister, Sheikh Hasina, for placing $100 million worth of aid funds into a spin-off organization of the bank called Grameen Kalyan. While this movement of money was explained as a way to decrease tax payments on the donations, the paper trail has not been transparent and, consequently, Grameen Bank and Yunus are experiencing negative attention for its microcredit activities. This has also called into question the unintended, destructive results of microcredit increasing suicides among those who cannot repay loans due to social pressures. Despite this recent backlash, the goal of microcredit continues to be increasing entrepreneurial practices at the most fundamental level for the lowest economic sector. This, in turn, raises the overall wealth of a nation, enhances education and business experience for women, and ultimately increases the lifestyle of the individuals and their families.

Xerox

Xerox traces its history of corporate venturing back to 1906, when the Haloid Company was incorporated to make and sell photographic paper. After decades of innovative distinction in the market, Xerox's competitive edge began to erode; the company faced losing $273 million in 2001.[11] As a result, Anne Mulcahy, then chief operating officer (COO), was appointed as the new CEO and led Xerox's return to the market with a competitive fervor. Contributing to Xerox's competitive edge were its acquisitions of companies with new technologies and access to customers that fit into the Xerox corporate strategy. Another way Xerox maintains its innovative edge is through its renowned R&D program.

Acquisitions play a major role in Xerox's corporate venturing model. The strategy gives Xerox access to both new customers and technology. Xerox spent $1.2 billion to acquire Global Imaging, an office equipment distributor. From the deal, Xerox gained access to 200,000 more customers. In early 2010, Affiliated Computer Services Inc. (ACS) was acquired, giving Xerox access to new business and government clients, technologies related to business process outsourcing and information technology services. In November 2010, Xerox acquired Spur Information Solutions, a company with software for parking enforcement.

Xerox's R&D program has long been the engine of growth for the company. R&D is so important to the company's long-term growth that in the face of enormous debt, Mulcahy and Ursula Burns (then COO and CEO) cut costs elsewhere in the company rather than subject its coveted R&D to shrinking budgets. The annual R&D budget at Xerox is around $1.5 billion. The Xerox Innovation Group comprises four research facilities. The facility in Toronto, Canada, works with materials; the facility in Grenoble, France, deals completely with intelligent documents; the facility in Rochester, New York, researches next generation systems; and the most well-known research facility, the Palo Alto Research Center (PARC), is located near Stanford University in California. This research structure has three roles. The first is the explorer role that involves fostering and pushing creativity to formulate innovative ideas. The second role is as incubator, where the ideas are analyzed in the labs to see whether they are appropriate for further company investments to bring to market. This essential role underscores the company's intrapreneurial spirit. The third role is a partnership role, whereby business group engineers have the challenge of formulating the idea into an actual service or product.

PARC plays a vital role in Xerox's innovative success; it is estimated that 95 percent of Xerox's products can be attributed to PARC. Researchers at PARC are given credit for inventing the personal computer, laser printing and the ethernet. Some of the researchers are referred to as 'work-practice specialists' who observe real life office operations and note where efficiencies can be made and new technologies introduced. This eclectic group of scholars includes scientists, engineers, anthropologists, physicists, artists and psychologists. Guiding Xerox's research function is what are referred to as the six S's: simpler, speedier, smaller, smarter, more secure and socially responsible.

Open face-to-face discussions on ideas are encouraged, and the researchers are also heavily involved in blogging and contributing to an intercompany wiki. Xerox strongly believes in creating the most conducive environment for creative thinking; the belief embedded within the company culture is that the best ideas and strategies do not come from top-down but from within. The culture encourages creative thinking, corporate entrepreneurship where employees are challenged to consider how the idea fits into the entire value chain, and loyalty and long-term vision for Xerox.

Google

Google is a good example of a company engaged in corporate venturing. Google has long invested in start-up companies. In March 2009, Google announced that despite the economic downturn, it was creating a $100 million venture fund to invest in exceptional start-ups in consumer internet software, biotechnology and healthcare. The company also invests millions of dollars in other projects that involve driverless cars, wind turbines and lunar robots. Google often invests in projects that do not seem connected to the company's core competencies in order to innovate in the industry's rapidly changing environment.

Google's corporate venturing spirit is rooted in innovation. Among the notable ways in which Google fosters the most conducive environment for creativity are:

- *Culture.* Google goes to great lengths to hire people who are the best fit for the company culture. They reward those who are the most capable and offer the best ideas. Risk taking, creativity and innovativeness are among the characteristics that help employees fit in at Google. The layout of the office design is to foster more communication among the employees. Google conducts Friday meetings where all employees meet over beer and are encouraged to speak candidly.
- *Budgeted time for innovation.* Technical employees are encouraged to spend 20 percent of their time on self-selected independent projects.[12] Even managers have time allotted to spend on special innovative projects. Managers spend 70 percent of their time on the core business, 20 percent on related but different projects and 10 percent on new businesses and ideas.
- *Qualification process.* Ideas are modeled, piloted and tested in controlled experiments before becoming authorized projects. The amount of time for an idea to become an authorized project is not long.
- *Crowd sourcing.* Google lets its users decide which products are best among a set of product offerings. The company strategy is to note the most useful ones and give them more development.
- *Tolerance for risk, failure and chaos.* In order to introduce innovative products, Google encourages risk taking. The company has a high tolerance for failure and chaos and hopes that Google employees learn quickly from mistakes and move forward with creating the next innovative products.

The cornerstones of the company's strategy are innovation, passion and risk taking. Indeed, Google is a good model of corporate entrepreneurship.

Implementing and evaluating a corporate venturing program

Implementing a corporate venturing program as well as evaluating results varies significantly by company depending on the organization's objectives. Some of the major issues include: determining the most appropriate corporate venturing model; committing the entire organization to the concept of corporate venturing for at least a three-year period; 'thawing' any 'frozen' obstacles (permafrost) in the organization that would inhibit corporate venturing; identifying corporate entrepreneurs; and developing an appropriate compensation scheme.

Implementing

As indicated in the examples in this chapter as well as in each of the chapters and chapter scenarios, there are many ways to implement and operationalize a corporate venturing program. A general approach, which can be tailored to the specific objectives of an organization, is indicated below.

Developing a corporate venturing program:

- Develop the vision and objectives of program with key members of the management team.
- Develop example(s) of the proposal to be submitted, establish the evaluation criteria and determine the amount of money available.
- Select members of the evaluation committee.
- Announce the start of the program with proposal submissions due in four to six weeks.
- Select winning proposals.
- Form venture teams.
- Communicate results and provide information on program internally throughout the company on a regular basis.
- Implement and structure the corporate venturing activity and climate.

Vision statement

The first step in the process is for the CEO and key members of the management team to develop the vision (mission) of the program. This is extremely important to avoid the syndrome, 'Without a detailed map, many roads will get you there.' Aspects of vision statements of several companies are indicated in Table 8.1. Some common elements in these mission statements are customer focus; quality product or service; employees are important; innovative activity; consistent quality delivery of product or service; and ethics and social responsibility.

Elements

Once the vision for the corporate venturing program has been established, several examples of a submission for support of a corporate venturing idea should be written. Ideally, these would be examples of the submission itself but at least should contain the elements needed. Having these examples will significantly increase the number of corporate entrepreneurship proposals received in companies being assisted by the author of this book. Also, the proposal evaluation criteria and the amount of money available should be determined.

Evaluation committee

A committee that will be evaluating the proposals needs to then be established. This committee needs to include an individual from each important functional area and should reflect some diversity in terms of position in the company. The CEO or head of the division should not be a member of the selection committee. Being a member of the committee compromises the ability of the CEO or division head to champion the entire program.

Program announcement

The next step is to announce the program throughout the company about four to six weeks before the proposal submission deadline. The announcement should include examples or elements of the submission required, the amount of money available, the evaluation criteria and the members of the evaluation committee. The proposal announcement should come from the highest level position in the group involved such as the CEO or division head and include an enthusiastic message encouraging every employee to participate. This support will significantly increase the degree of participation and the number of proposals submitted.

Table 8.1   Core of mission statements of selected US companies

3M	Innovation
	'Thou shalt not kill a new product idea'
	Absolute integrity
	Respect for individual initiative and personal growth
	Tolerance for honest mistakes; product quality and reliability
Ford	People as the source of our strength
	Products as the 'end result of our efforts' (we care about cars)
	Profits as a necessary means and measure for our success
	Basic honesty and integrity
General	Improving the quality of life through technology and innovation
Electric	Interdependent balance between responsibility to customers, employees, society and shareholders (no clear hierarchy)
	Honesty and integrity
	Individual responsibility and opportunity
Merck	'We are in the business of preserving and improving human life. All of our actions must be measured by our success in achieving this goal'
	Honesty and integrity
	Corporate social responsibility
	Science-based innovation, not imitation
	Unequivocal excellence in all aspects of the company profit, but profit from work that benefits humanity
Nordstrom	Service to the customer above all else
	Hard work and productivity
	Continuous improvement, never being satisfied
	Excellence in reputation, being part of something special
	Product excellence
Procter &	Continuous self-improvement
Gamble	Honesty and fairness
	Respect and concern for the individual
	'We exist to provide to our customers' – to make their lives better via lower prices and greater selection; all else is secondary
Walmart	Swim upstream
	Buck conventional wisdom
	Be in partnership with employees
	Work with passion, commitment and enthusiasm
	Run lean
	Pursue ever-higher goals

Proposal selection

At the same time as the winning proposals are selected and announced, carefully crafted letters indicating why other proposals were not accepted, along with encouragement to submit a proposal in the next round of proposals, should be sent to each individuals submitting a proposal that were not funded. Complete transparency is needed in the selection process in order to establish an environment that is very positive for the corporate venturing activities.

Venture team formation

When needed, the individuals with the winning proposals should be helped in their selection of a venture team. While assistance should be available, the corporate entrepreneur should make the final decision and ask whomever he or she feels would be a good team member. Alternative individuals should be identified, as usually some of the individuals asked will not want to participate. It is extremely important that no employee should be forced to participate as companies have experienced problems when this occurs.

Communicate results

In order for the corporate venturing process to become an integral part of the corporate culture, information on the activities of the funded venture proposals should be distributed regularly throughout the company. An internal company newsletter or at least email blasts are two means to accomplish this. Periodically, the CEO or division head should show support through the same medium. Successes should be celebrated.

Implement program

The second date for proposals should be announced at least four weeks before the due date; ideally, it would be announced along with the selection of the winning proposals of the first round. This enhances the acceptance of the program and makes it a regular activity of the company and part of the corporate culture. The author has had good success in implementing corporate venturing programs in both large and medium size companies using this approach. The actual corporate venturing program differed significantly by company, reflecting its vision and objectives.

Benefits of a corporate entrepreneurship program

The benefits of establishing and implementing a corporate venturing program are discussed in terms of benefits to the company and benefits to the employees.

Benefits to the company

The principal benefits of corporate venturing to the company are indicated below. One of the most important benefits is the increase in morale through the establishment of a new corporate culture. Employees will 'own their jobs' and want to make their positions operate in the best possible, most efficient ways. The new culture will make it fun for employees to come to work.

Benefits of corporate venturing to the company:

- establishing a new culture, better morale
- reduction in employee turnover
- motivated workforce
- new business concepts
- new ways of doing things
- more flexible organizational structure
- organizational learning
- positive impact on revenues and profits.

Employees liking what they do results in a reduction in employee turnover. Given the high cost of recruiting, hiring and training a new employee, higher retention rates result in substantial savings as well as retaining trained, experienced employees. Employees are motivated to make sure the company does as well as possible. Can you imagine the quality of output and performance that result from an experienced, motivated team? These highly motivated employees will contribute to an increase in revenues, reduction of costs and increase in profits. Corporate venturing provides new business concepts. These can include new products or services, better systems and new ways of doing things. These new ways of doing things will be the norm as employees are encouraged to try new things for the best performance of their positions. This will result in the company evolving into a more flexible organizational structure. There will be little or no turf protection, and teams can be easily formed to carry a project from start to finish. New products or services and new customers will occur and present customers will be more satisfied. With flexibility and newness constantly occurring, organizational learning will be an integral part of the company's operation. Learning results in employees being able to do multiple jobs, grow in their own competencies and increase the productivity of the company.

All these benefits will result in increased revenues and profits. New products or services, new customers and more efficient operations will reduce operational costs, increase revenues and increase profits.

Benefits to employees

The major benefits of corporate venturing to the employees are indicated below. With a flexible organizational structure and corporate entrepreneurial culture, employees will feel self-actualized. Experiencing self-achievement will in turn enhance loyalty, efficiency and performance.

Benefits of corporate venturing to the employee:

- feeling of self-achievement
- more job satisfaction
- increased skills
- financial and non-financial rewards
- excited to come to work
- able to be creative.

Increased job satisfaction is a common result of corporate venturing. With a culture of trial-and-error and try-and-experiment, employees actively make sure their jobs are done in the best possible way to the extent of being excited to come to work. This is perhaps the greatest benefit of corporate venturing for employees. Employees who are happy with their jobs and the company will make sure everything possible is done for the company to grow and prosper. With a learning organization operating, employees will increase their skills. And of course employees with increased skills feel better about themselves and their ability to perform better and more efficiently.

Financial and non-financial rewards will be given to employees involved. Performance-based pay rewards will regularly occur, as will non-financial rewards. Successful activities will be heralded, rewarded and made known throughout the organization. The trial-and-error culture will allow employees to be more creative and open to change the way their jobs are done, to invent new processes and to develop new products and services.

Evaluating the results

A company implementing corporate venturing needs to establish a system to evaluate the results. The author has had good success in establishing two overall evaluation procedures: benchmarking and measurements of output.

Benchmarking

In order to understand the impact of corporate venturing on the overall company culture, benchmarking should be done before the program starts, then every six months for the first two years and once a year starting in the third year. An overall benchmarking tool is indicated in Table 8.2. This table is composed of pairs of words or phrases that each person involved in the program should rate on a scale of 1 through 7. The author has tried variations of this scale, such as 1 through 5 and 1 through 9. One through 5 ratings do not give enough dispersion in the data, as individuals have the habit of avoiding the extremes, and 1 through 9 causes some confusion because of the nine points on the scale. A 1 through 7 scale provides a midpoint – 4 – where there is no opinion on the direction of the variable.

Table 8.2 Benchmarking cultural values and norms

Traditional organizational culture		Corporate entrepreneurial culture	Rating 1 through 7
Fragmentation	→	Wholeness	
Instruction	→	Vision	
Controlled	→	Freedom to act	
Dislike coming to work	→	Like coming to work	
Having no responsibility	→	Having responsibility	
Non-motivated	→	Enthusiasm and motivation	
Defined limits	→	Few barriers	
Limiting people	→	Growing people	

Table 8.2 shows some general pairs of variables to determine the impact of the corporate venturing program. These include such benchmarking variables as: instruction–vision; dislike coming to work–like coming to work; distrust–trust; and limiting people–growing people. Some, if not all, of these should be used along with any specific pairs of variables the company wants to use to measure any changes in the corporate culture. The more specific the pair of variables, the better. Launching and implementing a solid corporate venturing program causes a shift in the company from a traditional organizational culture to an entrepreneurial culture. The most significant change will occur in the first two years and should be measured twice a year.

Output measurements

A corporate venturing program should impact the operations of a company in addition to changing the culture. The following six measurements should be taken at the same time each year for the first two years, and once a year starting in the third year:

- amount of cost reduction achieved (currency)
- amount of increased revenue achieved (currency)
- employee turnover (actual number and percentage of workforce)
- customer turnover (actual number and percentage of customers)
- percentage of total company sales from products or services introduced in the last five years
- percentage of total company sales from new customers obtained in the last three years.

A company with a sound corporate venturing program should experience a decrease in costs, an increase in revenues, less employee turnover, less customer turnover, a higher percentage of sales coming from new products or services introduced in the last five years and a higher percentage of sales from new customers obtained in the last three years.

These benefits should start occurring in the second year of the program if not before. Some companies that the author has worked with have achieved positive results in the first year.

Summary

This chapter has focused on implementing a corporate venturing program. Following the introduction of five general models, some in-depth case histories of companies are discussed. A general implementation procedure is presented that can be modified for any company desiring to implement a corporate venturing program along with the benefits to both the company and the employees. The chapter concludes with a discussion of a benchmarking instrument and six measurements of output. Each of these should be administered to individuals participating in the corporate entrepreneurship program before the program begins and on a regular basis thereafter.

NOTES

1 Andrew Campbell, Julian Bradshaw, Andy Morrison and Robert van Basten Batenburg, 'The future of corporate venturing,' *MIT Sloan Management Review*, **45** (1), 2003, 30–37.

2 Robert Park and Andrew Campbell, *The Growth Gamble*, London: Nicholas Brealey International, 2005, pp. 10–32.

3 Jeffrey G. Covin and Morgan P. Miles, 'Strategic use of corporate venturing,' *Entrepreneurship: Theory and Practice*, March, 2007, 183–207.

4 Raghu Garud and Andrew H. Van den Ven, 'An empirical evaluation of the internal corporate venturing process,' *Strategic Management Journal*, Summer, 1992, 93–109.

5 William Buckland, 'Defining what corporate venturing actually is and what firms should do about it,' *Strategic Direction*, **19** (9), 2003, 2–4.

6 Robert A. Burgelman, 'A process model of internal corporate venturing in the diversified major firm,' *Administrative Quarterly*, **28**, 1983, 223–44.

7 Mark Gunther, Marilyn Adamo and Betsy Feldman, '3M's innovation revival,' *Fortune*, **162** (5), 2010, 73–6.

8 Ernest Gundling, *The 3M Way to Innovation*, Tokyo: Kodansha International, 2000, p. 46.

9 Gunther et al., '3M's innovation revival.'

10 Gundling, *The 3M Way to Innovation*, p. 46.

11 J.P. Donlon, 'The X factor,' *Chief Executive*, June, 2008, p. 234.

12 Bala Iyer and Thomas H. Davenport, 'Reverse engineering Google's innovation machine,' *Harvard Business Review*, April, 2008, 59–68.

Online sources

http://www.teslamotors.com/about.

http://www.bloomberg.com/research/stocks/snapshot/snapshot_article.asp.

Index

Academy of Achievement 58
ACNielsen 60
Advanced Ultraviolet Solutions
  acquired by Trojan Technologies Inc.
    114
Affiliated Computer Services Inc. (ACS)
  acquired by Xerox Corporation (2010)
    133
Airbnb 49
Airbus
  A340-300 28
  A340-600 28
Albright, Mark 60
alternative financial services (AFS) 47
Amazon.com 33
  internal politics in 108
  research teams 51
American Express Ventures
  as member of Dow Jones Industrial
    Average 42
  Centurion Card 44
  founding of (1850) 42, 52
  personnel of 52
  strategic investments made by 44
American Greeting Cards
  creativity practices of 32
American Research & Development
  acquired by Textron Ltd 88
Apple, Inc. 8, 14, 20, 44, 66, 70
  ApplePay 44
  acquisitions made by 67
  business plan of 67–9
    Network Innovation 68
    use in internal innovation 68
  creativity practices of 32
  iTunes 49–50
    store 67

personnel of 50, 66
product lines of
  Apple I 66
  Apple II 66
  Apple III+ 66
  Apple TV 67
  Emagic 67
  Final Cut Pro 67
  GarageBand 67
  iMac 67
  iMovie 67
  iPhone 32, 67, 130
  iPod 67–8
  Mac Operating System 8 67
  Powerbook G3 67
  Retail Stores 67
Aquafine Corporation
  acquired by Trojan Technologies Inc.
    (2005) 115
Argentina 76
attribute listing
  use in corporate entrepreneurship
    creativity 24
Austria
  Vienna 70
Avco Corporation
  acquired by Textron Ltd (1985) 88

Baby Boomers 51–2
ballast water treatment (BWT) 115
Bangladesh 131
Barclays 49
Bardhi, Fleura 48
BASF SE
  investments made by 132
Bayer AG
  Alka-Seltzer 77

Bell Aerospace 89
    acquired by Textron Ltd (1960) 88
    Bell-Boeing V-22 Osprey 90
    Model 429 90
Best Buy 60
Bezos, Jeff 33
Bic
    Bic Roller pen 76
bill.com 44
biofuel
    potential use in aircraft 28
Bladon, John 59
Blockbusters 30
Bloomberg 54
BMG 50
Boeing Company
    747 28
    787-9 Dreamliner 28
Bostich
    acquired by Textron Ltd 88
Boston Consulting Group 19
Boston Globe 57
brainstorming 21
    reverse brainstorming 21
Branson, Sir Richard 7, 27, 46
Burgelman, Robert A. 128
Burkart Manufacturing Co.
    acquired by Textron Ltd (1953) 87
Burns, Ursula
    CEO of Xerox Corporation 133
Business Insider 45
business plan 66–9
    corporate 71–3, 81–3, 86
        corporate fit 79
        executive summary 71
        market analysis 79
        market segmentation 79–81
        marketing plan 81–4
        plan for further action 85–6
        product/service analysis 71, 73–9
        profitability 84
    importance of 69–70
    scope and value of 70
business-to-business (B2B) 80
business-to-consumer (B2C) 79–80
business-to-government (B2G) 80
Business Week 58–7

Butterfield, John Warren
    role in founding of American Express
        42

Camcar
    acquired by Textron Ltd 88
Campbell, Andrew 126
Campbell, Lewis B.
    CEO of Textron Ltd 90–91
        role in establishment of TLT 90
Canada
    British Columbia
        Victoria 114
    Ontario
        London 113
        Tillsonburg 113
    Toronto 134
Cantillon, Richard 3
capital 6
    injection 27
Carnegie, Andrew 6
Carr, David 61
Carter, Jimmy 88
CBInsights 47
Center for Science in the Public Interest
    personnel of 53
Center for Sustainable Energy 54
Cessna Aircraft
    162 SkyCatcher 90
    acquired by Textron Ltd 89
charge cards 43
checklist method 26
    use in corporate entrepreneurship
        creativity 22
Chenault, Ken
    CEO and Chairman of American
        Express 52
Chevron Corporation
    corporate venturing efforts of 98–9
China, People's Republic of 30
Christensen, Clayton
    Innovator's Dilemma, The (1997)
        44–5
Chrysler
    Acustar Division 89
Church & Dwight
    Arm & Hammer Antiperspirant 76

Cisco Systems 98
  R&D efforts of 116
Coca-Cola Company 76
collective notebook method 26
  use in corporate entrepreneurship
    creativity 23
Collinson, Joseph
  Chairman and CEO of Textron Ltd 88
Computerworld 60
Container Corporation of America
  role in introduction of protective
    composite can 77
Cooper, Robert C.
  stage gate process of 39–40
corporate venturing 87–91, 111–12, 123,
    126, 129–30, 133, 136, 142–3
  benefits of 140–41
    for employees 141–2
  compensation of corporate
    entrepreneurs 117–18
    components of 119–20
    new success 120, 122
  evaluation of 142–3
    output measurement 143–4
  implementation of program 136–7,
    139
    communication of results 139
    elements 137
    evaluation committee 137
    program announcement 137
    proposal selection 139
    venture team formation 139
    vision statement 136–7
  internal 127
    models for 128–9
  internal politics 102–4, 108–9, 111–12
    concept of 103
    stinging 104
  joint 126
  leader characteristics 99–100
  leader selection 91, 98–9
  models of 126–9, 144
  obstacles 105
    human/non-human resource
      requirements 105
    legitimacy issues 105
    overcoming resistance 105–6

political strategies 106–7
  exercising of influence 110–11
  influence increase 109–11
survival guidelines 100–101
teams
  evaluation of performance 116–17
  roles 99
team selection 101
  venture life cycle 101–2
Coyne, Bill
  Head of R&D at 3M 130
Craigslist 60
credit cards 42
Crunchbase 49
CWC
  acquired by Textron Ltd 88

Daily News of Los Angeles 60
Danaher Corporation (DHR) 115
Daugherty, Paul 59
Dawning
  market shares of 30
DCA Food Industries Inc.
  financial incentives for personnel
    117
Del Monte Foods
  Del Monte Mexican Food 76
Dell, Michael 7, 33
Dell Computer 33
  internal politics in 108
Delta Airlines
  ownership stake in Virgin Atlantic
    Airlines 27
Denning, Steve 48–9
design thinking
  use in corporate entrepreneurship
    innovation efforts 35–7
digital video disc (DVD) 30
Diner's Club 43
disruptive innovation
  concept of 44–5
  influence of 45
Dolan, Beverly F.
  Chairman and CEO of Textron Ltd
    88–9
Donnelly, Scott C.
  CEO of Textron Ltd 90–91

Dos Equis
  advertising campaigns of 73
Dow Jones Industrial Average
  members of 42
Dr Pepper Snapple Group Inc.
  Schweppes Tonic Water 74
DuPont 14
Dyson
  research project methodology of 29

Eastman Kodak
  Kodak 75
eBay, Inc. 33
  disruptive effect of 60–61
  feedback forum 59
  founding of (1995) 58, 61
  personnel of 60
    research teams 51
Eckhardt, Giana M. 48
ecosystem venturing 126
Edison, Thomas 3, 6
Electric Light & Power 59
EMI Group Limited 50
entrepreneurship 1, 3
  corporate 1, 3, 6–8, 13–16, 25–6, 70, 91,
      98, 104, 106, 109–10, 117–18
    change 18, 24–6
    concept of 7–8, 18–19, 26
    creativity 18, 20–4, 26, 29–31, 40
    innovation 18–19, 26, 30–40
    ownership 18–20, 26
    value of business plan 70
  definitions of 3, 6–7, 9–10, 15–16
    behavioural attributes 7
    economic aspects 7
    innovation 6
  process of 6, 10–11, 13–14, 25–6
    determination/evaluation of
        resource requirements 10–12
    development of business plan 10, 12
    identification/evaluation 10–11
    implementation/management 10, 13
  social 1, 3, 16
    concept of 8–9
  technology 1
environmental containment treatment
    (ECT) 114

Ericsson
  development of 17–18
    acquisitions made by 18
    Ericsson Radio Dot System 18
    LM Ericsson AXE 17
  networks of 18
Ericsson, Lars Magnus 17
E-Z-GO
  acquired by Textron Ltd 90
  personnel of 88
  RXV 90

Facebook 33, 61, 83
  use of open registration policy 48
Fargo, William G.
  role in founding of American Express
      42
Fast Company Magazine 49
  Social Capitalist Awards 9
financial technology (FinTech) 47
First World War (1914–18) 43
Forbes 48
forced relationships 26
  use in corporate entrepreneurship
      creativity 23
Ford Motor Company
  corporate venturing efforts of 99
Forrester Research 51
Fortune 200 115
France
  Grenoble 134
free market 50
Frito-Lay, Inc.
  Cheetos 77
Fry, Art
  role in development of Post-it Note 99
FutureWorks 57

Gallup, Inc. 51
Gartner, Inc. 51
Garud, Raghu
  model for internal corporate venturing
      127
Gates, Bill 7
Genentech
  corporate venturing efforts of 98
General Electric (GE)

GE Aviation 28
  personnel of 91
General Foods 73
General Mills, Inc.
  corporate venturing efforts of 98
General Motors
  internal politics in 108
Germany 132
Ginsberg, Ari 8, 14
global system for mobile communication
    (GSM)
  introduction of (1999) 17
Goldman Sachs
  Global Investment Research 48
  use of stinging 104
Google, Inc.
  allocation of staff time for project
      research 29
  corporate venturing in 129–30, 134–5
  creativity practices of 32
  internal politics in 108
  research teams 51
Gordon method 22, 26
  use in corporate entrepreneurship
      creativity 22
Gorham
  acquired by Textron Ltd 88
governpreneurship 1
Grameen Bank
  corporate venturing in 129–30
  financial activity of 132–3
  microcredit model of 131–3
  recognised by Indian government
      (1983) 131
GTE Corporation 8
Guth, William 8, 14

Haloid Company
  incorporation of (1906) 133
Hardyman, James F.
  Chairman and CEO of Textron Ltd 89
  President of Textron Ltd 89
Harriman, Edward 6
Harvard Business Review 45
Harvard Business School 33
harvest venturing 126–7
Hasina, Sheikh 132

Henkel KGaA
  acquisitions made by 2
Hewlett-Packard (HP) 8
  corporate culture of 119
  market shares of 30
Homelite
  acquired by Textron Ltd 88

IBISWorld 56
Independent Electrotechnical
    Commission (IEC)
  InfoVision Award 18
India
  government of 131
  Jobra 131
industrial ultraviolet (UV) sector
    113–14
initial public offering (IPO) 59
Innosight 46
innovation venturing 126
Instacart 44
Intel Corporation 20
  corporate venturing efforts of 98
  internal politics in 108
  investments made by 132
Intercontinental Group 49
International Business Machines (IBM)
    Corporation 8, 66
  internal politics in 108
  market shares of 30
intrapreneurship 1, 7
Isaacson, Walter 50
Italy 17–18

Jacobson, Michael F. 53
James Bond (media franchise)
  Casino Royale (2006) 28
  Quantum of Solace (2008) 28
Japan 109
Jobs, Steve 7
  CEO and co-founder of Apple, Inc.
      50, 66
  refocusing of Apple business plan
      67–8
  removed as CEO (1985) 66
Johnson, Mark W.
  co-founder of Innosight 46

Johnson & Johnson
    Listerine household cleaner 76

K+S AG
    Morton Salt 75, 77
Kanter, Rosabeth Moss 33
Kazaa 49–50
Kelleher, Herb 32
Kellogg Company
    Pringles 77
Khatun, Sufia 131
Kimberly-Clark Corporation
    Kleenex 75
Kodak *see* Eastman Kodak
Krieble, Vernon
    founder of Loctite Corporation 1

Law, John 3
Lepore, Jill 45
Levi Strauss & Co.
    clothing lines of 76
LG-Ericsson 18
Little, Royal
    founder of Special Yarns Corporation
        (Textron Ltd) 87–8
Livingston, Fargo & Company 42
Loctite Corporation
    acquired by Henkel KGaA (1996) 2
    acquisitions made by
        Permatex 2
        Woodhill Chemical Sales Company
            2
    founding of (1953) 1
    product lines of 1–2
        Super Glue 1–2
Lucent Technologies 14

market disruption 45–6, 60–62
    market share ownership indicators 55
        CR4 concentration ratio 55
        Herfindahl–Hirschman Index (HHI)
            55–6
    public policy 50–53
        reactionary approaches 53–4
    societal/macroeconomic indicators 46
        access economy 48–9
        consumer white spaces 46–8

McDonald's
    franchise system of 33
McMurdy, Deidre 60
Mega-Cask 78
Mercedes-Benz
    dealerships of 33
Microsoft Corporation 66, 108
    corporate culture of 119
Miller, G. William
    President of Textron Ltd 88
Miller Brewing Company
    Lite Beer 73
Mondelez International
    Certs Gum 76
Morgan, John Pierpont 6
Moschella, David 60
Motorola, Inc. 66
Mulcahy, Anne
    CEO of Xerox Corporation 133
Musk, Elon
    founder and CEO of Tesla Motors 53,
        124

Napster 48–9
    clones of 49–50
Nash, Ed 50
National Automobile Dealers Association
    (NADA) 53
National Dry Cleaning Corporation
    bankruptcy of 58
Netflix 30
Netherlands, the
    Amsterdam 28
    Rotterdam 114
    Tilburg 125
New Republic, The 45, 61
New United Motor Manufacturing Inc.
    125
New York Stock Exchange (NYSE)
    87
New York Times 57, 61
New Yorker, The 45
NeXT 66
    acquired by Apple, Inc. (1996) 67
Nielson, Pete
    co-founder of Starlight
        Telecommunications 8

Nisen, Max 45
Nixdorf 14
Nokia Corporation 14, 117
  internal politics in 108
Nordic Mobile Telephone (NMT)
  inaugurated in Saudi Arabia (1991) 17
North Pacific Trust 6
Norway
  government of 132

O'Brien, William
  co-founder of Starlight
    Telecommunications 8
Omidyar, Pierre 59, 61
  founder of eBay 33, 58
    launch of feedback forum 59
OpenCEL
  acquired by Trojan Technologies Inc.
    (2011) 115
opportunity analysis plan 37
  structure of 37–9

Panasonic Corporation 125
parameter analysis 26
  use in corporate entrepreneurship
    creativity 24
PayPal Holdings, Inc. 44
peer-to-peer (P2P) finance 49
PepsiCo
  Pepsi Cola 76
Pfizer
  as member of Dow Jones Industrial
    Average 42
Pillsbury Company 77
Piper Jaffray consumer conference (2012)
  60–61
Polaris
  acquired by Textron Ltd 88
Polo, Marco 3
PriceWaterhouseCoopers (PwC) 49
private equity venturing 126–7
Procter & Gamble (P&G) 57–8
  as member of Dow Jones Industrial
    Average 42
  role in introduction of protective
    composite can 77
  Tide Dry Cleaners 56–7

Quaker Oats Company 73
  Aunt Jemima 75

Radius & RetailNext 44
Reckitt Benckiser Group
  Easy-Off window cleaner 76
Recording Industry Association of
    America (RIAA)
  estimation of digital music sales figures
    49
Republic of Ireland 2
research and development (R&D) 113, 126,
    130, 133
  external 116
Rifkin, Jeremy
  The Zero Marginal Cost Society 48
Roddick, Anita 7
Russian Empire 17

Sacks, Danielle 49
Salesforce.com
  research project methodology of
    29
Salsnes Filter
  acquired by Trojan Technologies Inc.
    (2012) 115
Satell, Greg 45
Sears, Roebuck and Co.
  internal politics in 108
  Kenmore 75
Second World War (1939–45) 43, 87
Sheaffer Pen
  acquired by Textron Ltd 88
Siemens AG 14
Silicon Valley 45, 61, 124
Singapore Airlines
  ownership stake in Virgin Atlantic
    Airlines 27
Skoll Foundation
  Award for Social Entrepreneurship 9
Skype 33
Smith, Adam
  Theory of Moral Sentiments 24
Sony Music Entertainment Inc. 50
South Africa
  housing availability gap in 47
Southwest Airlines 32

Speidel
   acquired by Textron Ltd 88
Spur Information Solutions
   acquired by Xerox Corporation (2010)
      133
Square 44
St Louis Post-Dispatch 57
St. Petersburg Times 60
Stanford University 134
Starlight Telecommunications
   founding of 8
Straetz, Robert P.
   Chairman and CEO of Textron Ltd 88
Swan, Bob 61
   Chief Finance Officer of eBay 60
Sweden 132

Taft, William Howard
   postal service legislation of 43, 52
Tektronix
   financial incentives for personnel 117
Telcordia
   acquired by Ericsson (2011) 18
telecommunications 17
   long-term evolution (LTE) 18
   telephone exchange (AXE) 17
      digital 18
   wideband code division multiple access
      (WDCMA) 18
Tesla, Nikola
   patent of AC induction motor (1888)
      124
Tesla Motors 53–4, 124
   facilities of 125
   lobbying efforts of 54
   Model 3 125
   Model S 124–5
   Model X 125
   motors
      85D 124
      P85D 125
   Powerwall 54
   Supercharger network 125
   Tesla Roadster 124–6
textiles 87
Textron Ltd 87
   acquisitions made by

AAI Corporation 90
American Research & Development
   88
Avco Corporation (1985) 88
Bell Aerospace (1960) 88
Burkart Manufacturing Co. (1953) 87
Camcar 88
Cessna Aircraft 89
CWC 88
E-Z-GO 90
Greenlee 90
Homelite 88
Lycoming Engines 90
Overwatch Systems (2006) 90
Polaris 88
Sheaffer Pen 88
Speidel 88
United Industrial Corporation
   (2007) 90
Valentine Holdings 88
divestitures of 89–90
founding of (1923)
   as Special Yarns Corporation 87
HR Textron 90
personnel of 87–90
revenues of 87–9
Textron Automotive Company 89
Textron Fastening Systems Inc. (TFS)
   89
Transformation Leadership Team
   (TLT) 90
Third Party Administration (TPA) 69
Thompson, Rupert
   CEO of Textron 88
Thorn EMI
   acquisition of Virgin Records (1992) 27
Toronto Stock Exchange 114
Toshiba Corporation
   corporate culture of 119
Toyota Motor Corporation
   corporate culture of 119
Traveler's Cheques 52
   provision of 43
Trinity College 1
Trojan Metal Products Limited
   acquired by Hank Vander Laan (1976)
      113

as Trojan Technologies Inc. 113
patents held by
    UV disinfection technology 113–14
Trojan Technologies Inc. 113
    acquisitions made by 114–15
        Advanced Ultraviolet Solutions 114
        Aquafine Corporation 115
        OpenCEL 115
        R-Can Environmental Inc. 115
        Salsnes Filter 115
        US Peroxide LLC 114
    facilities of 113–14
    R&D efforts of 113
Twitter 61, 83

Unilever
    investment efforts of 57
    Vaseline Intensive Care skin lotion 76
United Airlines
    corporate venturing efforts of 99
United Kingdom (UK)
    London 28, 59
        Gatwick Airport 28
        Heathrow Airport 27–8
    Manchester
        Airport 28
United Parcel Service
    corporate venturing efforts of 98
United States of America (USA) 42, 74,
        88, 125
    Austin, TX 53
    Bureau of Energy Statistics 51
    Bureau of Labor Statistics 51
    California
        Lathrop 125
        Palo Alto 66
        Self Generation Incentive Program
            (SGIP) 54
    Census Bureau 51
    Congress 53
    Department for Agriculture (USDA) 53
    Department for Justice (DOJ) 55
    Draper, UT 57
    Environmental Protection Agency
        (EPA) 126
    Federal Deposit Insurance Corporation
        (FDIC) 46–7

Federal Reserve 88
Food and Drug Administration (FDA)
    2
Hartford, CT 1
Immigration Department 42
New York, NY
    Rochester 134
Office of Personnel Management 51
Organic Foods Production Act (1990)
    53
Phoenix, AZ 70
Post Office 42–3
Seattle, WA 114
Smithfield, VA 75
Tucson, AZ 114
US National Highway Traffic Safety
        Administration 124
United Nations (UN)
    Human Settlements Programme (UN-
        HABITAT) 47
    Montreal Protocol (1989) 52
Universal Music Group 50
University of Hartford 47
US Dry Cleaning Corporation
    bankruptcy of 58
US Peroxide LLC
    acquired by Trojan Technologies Inc.
        (2004) 114

Valentine Holdings
    acquired by Textron Ltd 88
Van den Ven, Andrew H.
    model for internal corporate venturing
        127
Vander Laan, Hank
    acquisition of Trojan Metal Products
        Limited (1976) 113
Venmo 44
Virgin Atlantic Airlines/Virgin Atlantic
        Airways 28, 30
    aircraft fleet of 28
    launch of (1984) 27
    shareholders in 27
    travel class systems 27
Virgin Group
    creativity practices of 32
    expansion of 28

Virgin Records
acquired by Thorn EMI (1992) 27
Virgin Healthcare Foundation
'Change for Children Appeal' 28

Wall Street Journal 50, 57, 88
Walmart Stores, Inc.
corporate venturing efforts of 98
Walt Disney Company 109
Wampler, Jeff
CEO of Tide Dry Cleaners 56
Warner–Lambert
focus on speciality items 74
Warner Music Group 50
Wayne, Ron
co-founder of Apple, Inc. 66
Weiss, Mitchell D. 47
Wells, Henry
role in founding of American Express
42
Wells & Company 42
Wells, Butterfield & Company 42
Whitney, Eli 3, 6
Whole Foods Market 53
Wonder Bread
Advertising campaigns of 74
Wozniak, Steve
co-founder of Apple, Inc. 66

Xerox Corporation 8
acquisitions made by
ACS (2010) 133

Spur Information Solutions (2010)
133
compensation of personnel in 118–19
corporate venturing efforts of 99,
129–30, 133–4
personnel of 133
R&D program of 133
Palo Alto Research Center (PARC)
134
Xerox Innovation Group 133–4
Xerox New Enterprises 91

Yahoo! Inc. 98
Yunus, Muhammad 131
founder of Grameen Bank 131

Zennstrom, Niklas 33
Zoots
investments made in 57–8
Zuckerberg, Mark 33
Zuma, Jacob 47

3, network of 17–18
3M 8, 14, 20
allocation of staff time for project
research 29
corporate venturing in 129–30
Pacing Plus 130
creativity practices of 32
financial incentives for personnel 117
internal politics in 108
Post-it Note 99, 130

Titles in the **Elgar Advanced Introductions** series include:

International Political Economy
Benjamin J. Cohen

The Austrian School of Economics
Randall G. Holcombe

Cultural Economics
Ruth Towse

Law and Development
Michael J. Trebilcock and Mariana Mota Prado

International Humanitarian Law
Robert Kolb

International Tax Law
Reuven S. Avi-Yonah

Post Keynesian Economics
J.E. King

International Intellectual Property
Susy Frankel and Daniel J. Gervais

Public Management and Administration
Christopher Pollitt

Organised Crime
Leslie Holmes

International Conflict and Security Law
Nigel D. White

Comparative Constitutional Law
Mark Tushnet

International Human Rights Law
Dinah L. Shelton

Entrepreneurship
Robert D. Hisrich

International Trade Law
Michael J. Trebilcock

Public Policy
B. Guy Peters

The Law of International Organizations
Jan Klabbers

International Environmental Law
Ellen Hey

International Sales Law
Clayton P. Gillette

Corporate Venturing
Robert D. Hisrich